MW01031707

Tennis in the New Age: Ancient Knowledge and Modern Science

Tennis in the New Age: Ancient Knowledge and Modern Science

by Dr. Robert M. Soloway

SPORTS PSYCHOLOGIST

The Quest
Northboro, Massachusetts

COPYRIGHT © 2003 BY ROBERT M. SOLOWAY

ALL RIGHTS RESERVED. NO PART OF THIS BOOK MAY BE COPIED OR REPRODUCED IN ANY FORM OR BY ANY MEANS WITHOUT WRITTEN PERMISSION OF THE AUTHOR.

ISBN: 1-888861-09-6

Library of Congress Control Number: 2003090956

PRINTED IN CANADA

The Quest
P.O. Box 650
Northboro, MA 01532
800 777 9149
TheQuest@att.net
www.spiritwells.com

To all that sports has meant to me.

Introduction

Have you ever asked yourself what tennis training will be like in the future? I believe that tennis is heading down the path taken by modern medicine. For decades, Western doctors ignored ancient treatments like chiropractic, acupuncture, meditation, and herbal remedies. That changed only after their patients rebelled and began visiting alternative-medicine practitioners. In the United States today, people make more office visits to those practitioners than they do to conventional physicians. In Germany, St. John's wort, an herb, is prescribed nine times more often than Prozac for depression. In many countries, including the United States, hospitals are using acupuncture instead of anesthesia during certain operations. Meditation often is recommended as a treatment for heart disease, high blood pressure, and other stress-related illnesses. And several large pharmaceutical companies now have lines of herbal remedies. It seems that alternative has become mainstream.

Like New Age medicine, New Age techniques in sports training are derived from ancient wisdom, dating back thousands of years. Most of us are familiar with the ancient training techniques because of shows like "Kung Fu" and movies like *The Karate Kid*. The training is designed to help the participant develop mentally, psychologically, physically, and spiritually — the whole person. The ancient training produces athletes who are fit, focused, confident, and calm.

I began studying motor skills in graduate school, at about the same time I was introduced to Eastern philosophy via transcendental meditation. When I began to play tennis, I was fascinated with the mystical mental state players were calling *the zone*. Most people agree that being in the zone state produces optimal performance. As I played, I realized that I was having short zones — maybe one stroke or one approach-and-volley sequence that felt just right. I would hit a great shot; and immediately after found I was having two simultaneous reactions: delight with myself for hitting such a good shot and wonder. Did I really do that? I felt as though I wasn't fully conscious of what I had done, that I was playing "out of my head." Although I had thought about the shot, even planned it, I didn't feel fully responsible for executing the stroke. But if not me, who?

Of course I knew it was me, but I recognized a duality between my conscious mind, where thought dictates behavior, and my nonconscious mind, which controls my body almost instinctively. In a zone, your body seems to carry out its task on its own. You don't think about bending your knees or keeping your head down in a zone. No worries, doubts, or distractions get in the way of what your body does. Your mind sets the intention, but your body makes it happen.

Some call that almost-reflexive behavior *letting go*. The phrase implies a trust that the nonconscious mind will do what it has to do without conscious control. And some assign a magical, almost divine quality to the process. For them, letting go is a kind of surrender, and the nonconscious mind is the god within. *Trusting your nonconscious mind* may sound more psychological, and *zoning* may sound more hip. But it's hard to deny that there's something spiritual about letting go. That's why masters of kung fu and other martial arts are called *priests*.

Pretty soon, the mystery of zoning for me became "How can I do that again?"

The Western sports world, including the United States Tennis Association and its affiliates, seems convinced that zoning is an accident of factors: "You can't produce zones," the sports establishment insists. "Zones just happen."

Here's where Eastern philosophies enter the picture. Many of those philosophies believe that a zone is a state that can be encouraged, even induced, and that that is exactly the point of meditation, chanting, prayer, yoga, breathing exercises, and other rituals. In fact, the martial arts — among the world's oldest sports — have long recognized that zones occur naturally in physical activity and that it is possible to encourage zoning during that activity.

In the martial arts, the techniques that induce zoning are used to develop the whole individual: mind, body, and character. Students learn skill lessons and life lessons. In one "Kung Fu" episode, Master Po says to the young Caine, "That's right Grasshopper. The lion kills the lamb but honors it." His words are meant to develop the child's character, not his intellect or his physical prowess.

Why this emphasis on character, on personal development? What role do personality and attitude play in the induction of zones? Ultimately, knowing and trusting yourself are integral to the process: If you lack the wisdom to know yourself, your ability to zone is limited. Why? Because your conscious mind gets — or should I say *stays*? — in the way. There's a portion of your conscious mind that wants to take credit for your successes and to find explanations for your failures. Until you come to know yourself, your conscious mind is not going to trust your nonconscious mind to operate without supervision. And it's only when the nonconscious is allowed to function on its own that you can experience the zone state.

Zones exist; on that, everyone agrees. Is it possible to induce zones? Instruction in the martial arts proves it is. The question I asked myself: Can we apply the same techniques — the same focus on the development of self — to induce zones in tennis? My answer: a resounding yes. And this book describes the process.

There are all manner of lessons here: material that speaks to thinking about tennis and material that speaks to developing the skills of the game.

But the real value of *Tennis in the New Age* is its emphasis on character, the recognition that elements of personality can affect a player's game. Are you indecisive on the court? Are you passive? Do you lack focus or commitment? Do you procrastinate? If you answered yes to any of these questions, you're going to learn a great deal about yourself from this book, and your play will never be the same.

Know, too, that you may never be the same. Whatever you learn here about your attitude on the court, whatever you learn here about being calm or purposeful, you take with you. Zoning is a way to improve your performance in all of life's activities — from washing dishes to driving a car.

Certainly the methods described here transfer easily to other sports. In fact I would like to see them become part of a new model for training athletes, an acknowledgment that Western methods simply don't work for all athletes. I have seen such frustration on the faces of young players who've been told by their coaches that their only option in a given situation is a stroke that's not natural to them. It's not surprising that they stop enjoying tennis and even quit the game. People learn in all kinds of ways; it makes sense, then, to train athletes in all kinds of ways. Each of us has a unique style with which we can win. New Age tennis can help you find and bring out the best in you as a player and as a person.

This book describes an intensive weekend of training at a fictitious tennis academy called The Zone. I look forward to the day when places like The Zone are a reality.

Contents

List of Figures

Tennis in the New Age: Ancient Knowledge and Modern Science

The Recruitment Speech

As director of The Zone Tennis Academy, it's my job to bring our message to the public. I've given this talk a hundred times. At the moment, I'm listening to one of the coaches of a college tennis team as he introduces me, an introduction in which he overstates several of my accomplishments. I'm wondering where he got his information and deciding whether I should correct him. I don't think so. I'm so impressed with the person he's describing, even I want to hear myself talk.

Not so the young players. There are about twenty of them . . . with one bland expression. I know that today I might grab just one player's attention and change his or her life just a little. But that's enough. That's why I do it.

This group is going to get the middle-of-the-road talk. I have three that vary only by degree of spirituality. At the New Age Church last month, I talked about "Tennis for the Soul." Today, at the college, my topic is "Tennis in the Zone," and the part of God will be played by the nonconscious. Tomorrow I'm speaking at a country club on "Mentally Intense Tennis." *

The coach finishes up with my name: "So without further ado, here is Dr. Robert Soloway." There is no applause. They don't do that in college classes, at least not before the talk. When I give the talk at country clubs, they always applaud when I'm introduced, just to be polite. I like it. It wakes up the older folks who got there early and have nodded off.

"Good afternoon. I'm glad you're all here inside and dry. I like to think of myself as the best thing a tennis player can do on a rainy day."

I get a few chuckles. It's true, by the way. I made arrangements with the coach to talk to the team on the first rainy day of the semester. This coach wouldn't have given up a practice for a discussion on zoning. He's an old-timer who believes in hard work, great conditioning, and aggressive play. Right now he's sitting at the back of the room quietly going through a stack of papers. Here I am, a man with a Ph.D. in cognitive psychology coming to speak about motor-skill behavior, and the coach isn't even listening. A mental shrug — now I know what it must have felt like to be a chiropractor in 1950 — and I continue.

* We make clear to participants in this training that they will hear talk of spirituality but not religion. We don't make references to a particular god; instead we talk about universal laws and natural order. We also make clear that students who are uncomfortable with talk of spirituality can approach the lessons from a scientific or psychological context.

THE RECRUITMENT SPEECH

"Some of you probably think napping is the best thing a player can do on a rainy day."

More chuckles. I wander over and stand near a student who's sleeping. "Some of you are obviously planning to combine the two."

Lots of chuckles. The groggy student shakes himself awake. "Most good tennis players, like participants in any sport who have achieved a moderate level of expertise, know the state of mind called the *zone*. Have you all heard of it? Have any of you experienced it?"

All of the students nod.

"In other sports, it's called *being on, in the groove, a runner's high,* or *feeling it*. Coaches, trainers, and sports psychologists all agree that when players are in a zone, their performance is at its best. So if players in a zone play so well, why don't coaches teach players how to get into a zone?"

I thought that would get the coach's attention. It didn't.

"The answer is simple. Lots of coaches believe that a zone is an altered state of mind that players stumble into by chance, when everything seems to be going just right, and that there is nothing they can do to increase the likelihood of zoning. But they've got it backwards: The zone comes first, and then things get going right. And, more important, you can increase the likelihood of zoning."

I walk back to the groggy student; he's asleep again.

"Think about sleep for a moment." The other students laugh, but he sleeps on.

"It's a naturally-occurring altered state. You can't force yourself to sleep, but you can set up conditions that make it easier for you to sleep."

I point to the student's feet on the chair in front of his own: "You lie down."

I point to the cap pulled down over his eyes: "You make it dark and tune out other stimuli."

I roll my eyes, and the students laugh. The sleeping student wakes up. I greet his arrival with "Thank you."

As a buddy fills him in, I go on: "In the same manner, you can't force yourself into a zone, but you can set up the conditions in which you are more likely to fall into a zone.

"Before we get too far along, I want to define what we're calling a *zone*. The great golfer Bobby Jones is credited with saying, 'When I am playing well, I think of one thing; and when I'm playing really well, I think of nothing.' It's that *thinking of nothing* that seems to be the subjective experience of the zone state in tennis and other activities. I have a friend who says that when he's in a zone, he's playing 'out of my head.' In actuality, he's still in his head; he's just out of his conscious mind. When you're playing in a zone, you're playing nonconsciously.

"Let's talk about animals for a minute. When a monkey swings through the treetops, it never thinks, 'I can't do this.' The animal knows exactly what it wants to do — get from here to there — and does it. Animal performance is so high because animals are always in a zone. They don't have the disadvantage of conscious thoughts that produce things like worry, fear, and self-doubt.

"Now think about you. When you're on the court, have you ever said to yourself, 'Uh-oh, another backhand' or 'Oh no, another overhead'?"

Lots of heads nodding.

"It's those types of thoughts that keep you from playing your best. The conscious mind is both blessing and curse. With our conscious mind, we have created all manmade wonders, including tennis. But the conscious mind is also the source of our insecurities and anxieties.

"Now, think about it: It couldn't possibly require conscious thought to perform a motor skill well. If it did, how would animals manage?

"Reading provides a good example of the difference between performing a skill consciously and nonconsciously. Some readers are *decoders:* They read by sounding out words and then construct meaning by memorizing what they've read, by consciously processing the words. Decoders usually read slowly and comprehend very little, and most don't enjoy reading.

"For others, reading is a joy. The meanings of the words jump off the page at them, and they can get completely involved in what they're reading. The process is easy and fast . . . and nonconscious. In fact, much like athletes in a zone, good readers often lose track of time: They can get lost in a book for hours."

I pause and look around at the students. "How many of you read that way?"

Fewer than half the students raise their hands.

"Well, you may not fall into a zone when you read, but all of you have been there and not just on the tennis court. It might happen while you're working at a job you love or painting a picture or playing music. Only when you're done do you realize how focused you've been and how quickly time has slipped by."

I hold up a poster titled "What Is a Zone Like?":

- The participant is very involved in what he or she is doing to the exclusion of other stimuli or distractions.
- The participant's perception of time is distorted: Hours may pass like minutes.
- The participant's performance is excellent and very creative.
- Although the participant has been very productive or creative, he or she has few specific memories of the time spent in the zone.
- The participant feels less stress and anxiety.
- The participant may be working hard but has no sense of that: The difficult seems easier.
- The participant remembers the zone state as enjoyable time.

"These are the common characteristics of a zone," I say and then read each item aloud.

"Many people think that these modes — on and off the athletic field —

are just fortuitous, that we can't make them happen. But practitioners of meditation, yoga, tai chi, and many of the Eastern martial arts are able to achieve zone states *intentionally*. And in some of these activities, achieving the zone state is the participants' primary goal. They hope that by repeating the zone state in their practice, they will be able to achieve the zone state in all areas of their lives.

"In the East, living full-time in a zone is called *enlightenment,* and that's what these practitioners are working toward. They believe that the more you zone in your practice, the more likely you are to zone in life. In other words, falling into a zone makes falling into more zones easier.

"Notice that the practice — the discipline in which you learn to zone — can be meditation or exercise or even martial arts. Whatever the skill, the study of that skill includes the study of a philosophy of life and a spiritual practice. Have you ever seen the old TV show 'Kung Fu'? The young Caine had studied to be a Shaolin priest. Doesn't it seem odd that the method of training a priest was to make him an expert at fighting? But the fighting is incidental: The zoning is everything. Remember Mr. Miyagi in *The Karate Kid?* Like Caine, he was calm, wise, and confident. And like Caine, he had learned to zone through the practice of fighting.

"In the West, we teach motor skills as activities for the body alone. We break down a skill into its components, teaching each component in turn: Bend your knees; keep your wrist firm. Kung fu masters don't practice breathing, kicking, or contorting the body to perfect their breathing, kicking, or bending. Physical skill is just one path to enlightenment, and excelling at a physical skill is just a by-product of the journey."

Now comes the sell.

"I teach tennis, but what I really teach is self-discovery. Remember: The game is incidental; the zoning is everything. As you learn more about yourself, your tennis will improve in wonderful ways: You'll be calm, highly focused, and confident — a tennis master. Of course mastery won't happen overnight, but you should begin to see change in your performance very quickly. Even better, you'll find yourself enjoying the sport more. Thank you."

Now the students applaud. The coach looks up and joins right in, never having heard a word. He stands and asks for questions. This is where I find out if anyone's been listening.

A young woman raises her hand.

"Will people be able to see that you're doing something different? Like with your eyes or something?"

"Well, once players are trained this way, they become much better at tracking the ball, and you can see a kind of intensity in their eyes. They also tend to make sort of a funny face." I tighten my mouth and squint. Then I laugh and say, "Not really. I think they just look more intense."

Another young woman raises her hand.

"Hi. I read some of your book. You seem to say that your personality is in your tennis game."

Several of the guys rib her for brownnosing. She continues: "Like what do you look for? How can you tell?"

"We usually let the person help us find it. You probably know the kinds of things you do to shoot yourself in the foot, not just on the court but in other areas of your life too. Let me ask you something: How do you act when you have something difficult to say? Suppose a friend borrowed money from you last month and still hasn't paid you back and you need it. What do you? Do you put off asking? Do you worry about what to say or even practice what you're going to say? Do you plan it at all?"

"I usually just blurt it out as fast as I can. I don't like thinking a lot about things."

"No kidding!" one of the other players comments, and several others laugh.

I turn to the student who called out: "What did you mean when you said that?"

"Well, Marla is like a free spirit. She's, she's . . ."

"Spacey!" another student calls out.

Most of the students are smiling. Even Marla is nodding her head.

I turn back to Marla: "Is that a side of you? Are you spacey?"

"I guess so," she answers.

"Is it a part of your game?"

"It was yesterday," jokes the same friend.

Marla concedes: "I guess I could be more focused."

"Well that's what we'd help you to see. If you aren't being all you want to be because you're acting spacey, then spaciness is how you shoot yourself in the foot, and you do it on the tennis court as well. If we can help you see how your spaciness affects your tennis and your life, then I think you might be motivated to be a little less spacey. We have ways of helping you focus while you're playing. Together, you wanting to be less spacey and the staff helping you get over it, we can really make a difference. It only takes a small change in a single trait to make a big impact on your game."

Marla looks satisfied with my answer. I think she'd like what we do.

THE RECRUITMENT SPEECH

Orientation

From my office window I can see the new arrivals getting out of the rickety bus that brings them here from civilization. Some clearly are not thrilled with our less-than-elegant facility, but that's all part of the program. It's an environment in which they can change. We think of it as rustic.

We haven't had a group this highly touted in some time. The ranked players are always the most challenging: They have the most to lose by changing their game.

I watch the bus leave, belching and groaning its way up the hilly road. It had been so quiet as it coasted downhill that I assumed they finally fixed it. But at the first point of challenge, the bus reveals it's still struggling with the same problems. "Just like people," I think. "We all look pretty good when we're coasting, when we're cruising along."

As director of The Zone, I am expected to see the players as they really are. To do that, I have to challenge them. Without the challenge, they would reveal as little as the bus coasting downhill.

These players and their families sought us out. They have expectations.

But this isn't an ordinary school. We discourage expectations. Instead, we try to be just what they need.

●

Discussion at dinner was lively, a good sign. I hope the students like to talk in class. The lessons flow so much better when there is participation. Of course, sometimes silence can be powerful too. A shy student is much more likely to open up and share in a quiet class.

Friday evening is always special. There's an excitement to it. Part of it is the newness and the nervousness that goes with that. Part of it is the exchange of energies that is about to occur as this group of strangers goes through a process together. The mix of personalities is always unique, yet magically just right for everyone's needs to be met. Sometimes the first night we can see a scenario beginning to take shape. There may be a jokester in the crowd and someone else who is very serious about what's going on. The first night, the two grate on each other's nerves. But by the end of their visit, each is grateful for the other because they've come to understand that that's how lessons are learned.

We take sixteen students at a time, sometimes dividing them into two groups of eight. Sometimes eight are hitting while eight are in class.* We find the smaller number more intimate. With some groups, we do more separating; with others, less. We don't plan it. In fact we try not to plan any of the specifics: Part of the training is learning not to sweat the details of your performance. With that pep talk to myself, I head in to meet the new group.

---

* Time at The Zone is split between classroom and court. We call the class time *lessons* and the court time *sessions*.

Lesson 1

The classroom is small. There are no chairs. The floor is carpeted, and there is an assortment of pillows, cushions, and ottomans. We make certain everyone is comfortable. A few students aren't used to sitting on the floor, but breaking patterns is part of the program. The lighting is soft — enough for taking notes but far from bright.

I walk in, say hello, and introduce myself. Then I hand a sheet of paper to each student. "Before we begin, I'd like you to write down at least five weaknesses in your tennis game. Be as specific as you can. Don't just write down 'backhand' if you know what it is about your backhand that's a problem. Note the problem: 'I hit my backhand too close to my body,' for example. If it's a style thing — like 'I hate to go to the net,' write that and any reason you can think of — like 'because I hit short approach shots.' If it's something that happens only in matches — 'I double-fault in tiebreakers' — then write that. Got it?

"While you're writing, I'd like to share a little background about the process we use here. I'm almost embarrassed that I stumbled on the best

READER: **Please write down a description of at least five weaknesses in your game.**

16

part of the technique by accident. I knew that thinking 'Uh-oh, here comes a backhand' wasn't what I wanted to be thinking while I was playing, but I wasn't sure what I *should* be thinking. When you're learning a sport, no one ever tells you what your mind should be doing.

"After worrying about it for a bit, I realized that I needed to be concentrating, so I began looking for a way to increase my concentration, my focus. When I was in graduate school, I had done some research into imagery training in motor skills. Usually the skills used in this type of research are dart throwing or foul shooting — for the obvious reason that improvements are easy to track. What if I could create some type of imagery training that would keep tennis players focused on their game?

"So, several years ago, I began developing an imagery technique — it's gone through many refinements — that has been very effective in helping players focus. It demands sharp attention and clear intentions.

"The better I became at focusing, the more I began to realize that certain psychological barriers were interfering with my ability to concentrate, that they were preventing me from achieving my potential. So we incorporated attitude in the training here. We believe that if you have difficulty with a certain stroke or trouble winning matches with lesser opponents, it's not a problem with some misbehaving body part. It's a problem with your attitude. And chances are, that attitude is keeping you from being all you can be in other areas of your life as well. I'll bet if you have trouble coming to the net, you also have trouble asking for a date or a raise.

"So, your tennis game reveals a difficulty. We use that information to address the problem — to change the stroke or the outcomes of matches — by examining and changing the player: you. We change the way you play by helping you change your attitude.

"An example: If you tend to procrastinate off the court, I bet you find it hard to serve and volley, or to chip and charge the net. These are behaviors that people who procrastinate don't do naturally. If they did, they wouldn't be procrastinators. You and your game are inextricably linked. If you change your attitude, you change your game.

"Two elements, then, form the basis of New Age tennis. You must have sharp focus and the right attitude. And the best news — this is the part I stumbled on — is that together sharp focus and right attitude induce zoning. The more you zone, the better your performance on the court and elsewhere. And there's a bonus: the calm, the confidence, the focus, the fun, and the spiritual growth that are part of the zoning experience.

"Of course, in this country, most coaches and trainers teach only the physical part of motor skills. Certainly the local tennis pros were completely baffled by the concept, that zoning could increase players' concentration, change their attitudes, and improve their play. There seemed to be a need for a place to teach New Age tennis, and so here we are."

I pause and look around the classroom. "Okay, is everyone done writing down five or more difficulties in their game? Now put the papers aside, but don't lose them.

"Before we begin tonight I just want to be sure that you understand zones. Let's talk for a minute about how they happen in everyday life. And they do . . . naturally and frequently. You go to the school gym to help make and hang decorations for a dance. You get there at seven, and you're given a job to do. The next thing you know, it's ten o'clock. You've been working for three hours, but the time has just flown by. You know you were busy; you know you were enjoying the work. But you don't really remember exactly what you were doing or exactly what everyone said during that three hours. You were productive; you can see that the group did a great deal of work; and you remember that the team effort felt terrific. But you don't have specific memories of the time. Why? Because you were in a zone. That's your first lesson. You have to be into it, whatever it is. You can zone in any activity, as long as you're into it.

"Can any of you think of a team project that you remember this way?"

A hand goes up, and a student answers: "Yeah. I've even had that kind of experience doing disgusting things, like plumbing stuff or digging fence holes or painting. Somehow it doesn't seem so bad while you're doing it if you have a partner or a team effort going."

I love those kinds of comments.

"That's exactly what I mean. You can zone doing anything. Another example: Who loves to read? I see some of you nodding your heads. I bet there are times when you get lost in a book. You start reading, and suddenly it's two hours later. You've read and understood a whole bunch of pages. Do you remember turning each page? No. Do you remember exactly what was on each page? No. But you know that the time was spent productively, that you were focused, undistracted, and that you were enjoying the experience. You were in a zone.

"And that's the second lesson: Zones are enjoyable. Whether you lose yourself in a conversation, in a computer game, in an art project, or playing the violin — for me, it's my writing — you enjoy the experience. That enjoyment, the pleasure in a really great performance, is what draws us to our zone activities. You might feel addicted to tennis. For others it might be music, art, writing, or jogging. Whatever it is, we feel that we have to do it. And in some sense we do. We need those zones.

"I think of zones as a level of consciousness. In my somewhat simplified hierarchy, there are five levels of consciousness." I point to a poster on the wall.

"Most of us experience four of these five states on a regular basis. Everyone is familiar with the first three. Within those states are enormous variations. Sleep can be very light to very deep, and it may or may not involve dreams. The dream state is interesting because it includes all of the dreams we have at night and all of our daydreams as well. There are many different kinds of wakefulness too, among them arousal, relaxation, and anxiety.

"The fourth state, transcendence, is a temporary zone state. The zone may last for a moment or a few hours, but it is fleeting.

Levels of Consciousness
1. Sleep
2. Dreaming
3. Wakefulness
4. Transcendence
5. Enlightenment

"All zones have certain elements in common. We've talked about several of them: the focus, the absence of distractions, the sort of quieting of the conscious mind, the compression of time, the enjoyment. The primary difference is the source: Some zones are produced by physical activity, by playing tennis or running; others, by the absence of activity, through meditation, for example. That difference is reflected in the visible characteristics of the zone: A tennis player in the zone may be swinging her arms or pumping his fists — Jimmy Conners comes to mind; on the court we don't find the peace and calm we associate with meditation. But internally, both player and meditator are functioning nonconsciously: They are both very much 'out of their heads.'

"In a few minutes we're going to do a meditation exercise to help you understand a common thread of zoning, the settling down of the conscious mind. That understanding is going to help you start noticing all of the zones you fall into in your life.

"Finally, the highest level of consciousness is enlightenment. At this level, you're permanently zoned. Your actions are spontaneous, in the moment, confident. You're like Caine in the TV show 'Kung Fu': very alert, very calm, very creative, very effective, very at peace.

"There is general consensus among Eastern philosophies that zoning begets zoning, that the more you zone, the more likely you are to zone spontaneously. It makes sense, then, to notice the activities you do that induce zones, like reading or listening to music, and see to it that you work as many of those activities as possible into your day. We do know that over time, people who meditate regularly begin to experience a meditative calm spontaneously in other activities, including tennis. That's why we begin each lesson with a meditation exercise.

"By the by, if the word *meditation* bothers you, call it a *breathing exercise* or *relaxation technique*. There is nothing inherently spiritual about the technique. In fact, you'll find the technique useful as a relaxation tool during matches."

I ask if everyone's comfortable with the idea of meditation. No one in the group seems troubled.

"Here's the method I teach. You're going to focus on your breathing, but in an unusual way. I want you to breathe in one nostril and out the other, and then breathe in the same nostril and out the first. Keep repeating: in the right, out the left, in the left, out the right. Don't use your fingers or anything else to block your nostrils. Just concentrate on the pattern. And don't try to control your breathing; just follow it. That means if you feel like taking a long deep breath, take it. If you're breathing slowly or quickly, it doesn't matter. You're not trying to alter the amount of air you breathe or the rate at which you breathe it, just which nostril it comes in.

"While you're doing the exercise, if a thought comes to mind just let it be. Don't pay it any attention, and don't try to ignore it. Just leave it alone and continue breathing in the pattern. Will you be able to control the flow of air into the 'correct' nostril? It doesn't matter. What matters is your intention to do it. Are there any questions?"

I get a couple of hands. I point to a middle-aged woman.

"I've seen people hold their hands like this," she says, her left hand palm up with thumb and index finger forming a circle. "Does that have some special meaning?"

"I've heard that it's supposed to activate a higher part of the brain. Remember that the opposable thumb is one of the physical characteristics that separates human beings from other animals. I think if it feels good, do it; if you have to strain to remember to do it, don't do it."

"What if one nostril is clogged?" asks a young man.

"Good question. I think you'll find that this exercise will open up your passageways, but don't ever force air out of a nostril. Just breathe easily, and if you have to use your mouth as sort of a release valve, that's okay. Just follow the rhythm of your breathing. Don't try to control it."

I look around. "Any other questions?" There are no more hands. "Okay, now, I want you to be comfortable. Lean up against the wall or cross your legs, whatever, just get comfortable. But don't lie down. When you lie down, you're telling yourself that you're intending to sleep. You want to use a different position for meditating. You want to alert your mind that a different state is coming.

"We're going to do about eighteen minutes. I'll keep track of time, so you don't have to. Remember: in one nostril and out the other, and then in the

READER: **Please join in. Do about eighteen minutes. If you do more or less, fine. Don't get bent out of shape over time. If you have some place to be after the exercise, set an alarm and forget about the time.**

same nostril and out the first. Just breathe at your natural rate, and leave your thoughts to themselves. Are you ready? Close your eyes and begin."

At this point, we all meditate for eighteen minutes — me too. That's the best part of teaching meditation: I get to meditate. I guess if you teach cooking, you get to eat. Maybe all teaching has its fringe benefits.

After years of meditating, I just know when the eighteen minutes are up. In the classroom, though, I always check myself against my watch. I go on: "Now take a minute, and come out slowly. Open your eyes gently. Give yourself a chance to gather."

I wait about a minute for everyone to come back. "How was that? Relaxing? Calming? Look around at your classmates. See the peace in their eyes? Feel the quiet?"

As they look around from face to face, they can't help but smile at the shared experience. It's almost like the closeness that develops between strangers who have traveled together. The exercise unifies the group. Somehow meditating together is a bonding experience.

I ask: "Did any of you fall into a zone?"

Several students nod, and several others murmur yes.

One student calls out: "Not the whole time, though."

I say, "That's okay. Almost no one zones the whole time. After all, you were concentrating on your breathing in and out, and I'm sure you had thoughts about all kinds of things. But trust me. Several times, for seconds or even a minute, you drifted away and forgot the technique, and your conscious mind stilled. Those moments are hard to catch because when you're in a zone, you're not thinking.

"The way you usually know you've had a zone experience is realizing that you've been thinking about something else, not the breathing technique, and that you don't remember when you stopped the breathing technique or how you started thinking about whatever you caught yourself thinking about. In between breathing in and out and catching yourself thinking about something else, you zoned out. You simply weren't there for a moment. In a sense, you've lost that moment. You feel certain you weren't sleeping; you just weren't thinking about anything.

"The technique works by focusing on one thing: the breathing instructions. As the breathing becomes routine, your mind quiets down and you're likely to fall into a zone. You'll use the same process on the tennis court. You're going to be focusing on just one thing — your targets — and as that becomes routine, you'll find yourself more likely to fall into a zone.

"Remember: Zoning begets zoning. The more zones you experience intentionally, the more zones you'll experience spontaneously. Of course you can't skip life to sit and zone all day; but you can try to add zones to your life. Both this breathing technique and the tennis technique we teach should help you increase the number of zones you have.

"A zone in some ways is our natural state. In a zone, you perform by instinct, the way animals do. But even if your brain is working at a lower level, that doesn't mean that you're performing at a lower level. What the absence of conscious thought and analysis does mean is that you perform worry-free and easily.

"I take my dogs to a park where there's a makeshift bridge over a small stream. I've watched people of all ages cross the bridge with caution. My dogs run across it happily. Of course, we can't have exactly the same mental experience that animals do. We're humans, and our minds work differently. But humans do have the ability to witness, to be involved in what's going on without consciously being attached to it. That's a common experience among top tennis players.

"You can see when a zone kicks in. Those players are so focused that they're not seeing or hearing the crowd. They are so connected to their game that they're not simply hitting a passing shot, they *are* the passing shot.

"We're all capable of performing in a zone state. In fact, we're all capable of living in a zone state. It's an ability that develops over time, but it's time well spent. Thank you."

A few of the students applaud. The group seems very receptive.

Session 1

"We begin tonight with an exercise to see how well you target your strokes. While you're hitting, I want you to see how often you actually create a precise shot in your head. Don't worry about volleys that happen too quickly or bad bounces or balls your opponent has struck particularly hard. Those are difficult shots to aim consciously. Focus instead on your usual strokes, and with each stroke ask yourself, 'Did I have a target?'

"Here's what I want you to do. Rate the clarity of your target on every stroke from zero to three. Zero is no target at all: You're just trying to hit the ball back. Rate the shot a one if you have a vague idea of what you're aiming for — you know, 'over there somewhere'; a two if you have a general idea of stroke and location — 'hard and deep in that corner'; and a three if your target is very clear — 'with topspin to that precise spot.'

"A few things to remember: Don't fib. You'll find that you target certain strokes better than others. That's exactly the kind of information we're looking for. Also, timing counts. If you think a target but aren't focusing on it at the moment you swing, that's a zero. Early targets are better than none, but in terms of occupying your conscious mind, the moment you swing is crucial. Finally, don't try to change anything about your play at this point. We just want to get an idea of how well you target now, before we begin training.

"Okay, we're going to pair you off to hit. As you hit each stroke, immediately call out the number you give it. Don't wait to see how well the stroke works. If you think you've hit a three, call it out. Even if the ball goes over the fence, it's still a three. We're not scoring performance here, just how well you think you're targeting. Any questions?"

A young woman raises her hand: "What if you have to run really far to get a ball?"

"And what? You don't make a target when you're running?" I ask.

"Well, sometimes I just can't think about what I'm going to do because I'm so busy scrambling."

"If you're not thinking about a target when you swing, then you'd rate the shot a zero. We need to know what you're thinking with every shot. So you need to rate every shot except the balls that bounce funny. Okay?"

There are no more questions. We pair the students off and let them rally while they call out the numbers. While they're hitting, I walk around with several instructors and watch each player. We have a checklist we use to record each player's targeting numbers on many different kinds of strokes (Figure 1). As soon as we feel we have an accurate picture of a player, we move on to another player. Often we have to shuffle players to see a

Figure 1
Targeting checklist

Stroke	Scores	Notes
Name: Marla Fazio		
Approach	1101022110	Forehand, backhand about the same
Backhand	2212323132231223112	Better on slow balls
Forehand	2223232323233333222 3	Targets better when still and hitting motionless
Lob	1211221	
Overhead	22212233232	
Passing shot	1211221	Lower number when pressured
Put-away	233232333	Very sure here
Serve	3332323323223323 33332	
Volley	111121111121	Forehand, backhand the same

particular stroke — passing shots, for example — or we might even ask a player to hit a certain stroke.

About half the players become aware of their patterns; the rest don't. Of course, when they're playing, they don't hit just one kind of stroke in a row. They may hit one or two volleys and then another volley a few minutes later, which makes seeing a pattern more difficult.

After we've evaluated the students' targeting abilities, they begin playing games. We assign them to the courts based on what seems to be their skill level: the weakest players on the first court, the strongest players on the last. As they compete, the winners move up a court and the losers move down; the weakest player and the strongest player stay where they are. After they've warmed up, the students play six games or until the whistle blows. Service is determined by racket spin. As they play, the instructors make notes about different aspects of each player's game. It takes each instructor about two hours to evaluate four players. Here, too, we move the students around if we have to to see the full range of their games. And if we don't have what we need — say a strong serve-and-volleyer — one of us gets into the game.

We take lots of notes about each player's swing and game. What kind of things do we look for?

● Obvious problems with one or more strokes and the source of those problems.

Figure 2
Hitting the ball

a. Timing: early or late

b. Distance from the body: too close or too far

c. Racket height: high or low

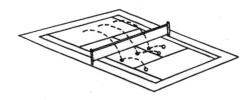

d. Bounce: on the rise, at the top, or falling

- Quirks, unusual stances or grips, and other distinguishing characteristics.
- For each stroke, whether the ball is hit (a) early or late; (b) too close or too far from the body; (c) with the racket held high or low; (d) or on the rise after the bounce, at the top of the bounce, or when the ball is falling (Figure 2).
- Where the player likes to hit the ball when returning service or hitting overheads.

- Stance: the distance between the player's feet and the position of the player's feet in relation to the net (vertical or more horizontal). Also whether the player's feet are moving when he hits the ball.
- The player's knees: Does she bend them? When? For what strokes? In what situations?
- Style weaknesses: Does the player avoid the net? Does he seem to have trouble with a certain kind of opponent? When does his game fail? What does it look like when it does? How does he act when his game is off?
- We ask about previous coaching. If a coach has told a player to take a fuller backswing on her forehand, we write it down. Or if a problem has been coached out of a player — letting overheads bounce, for example — but still shows up occasionally, we write it down.

Basically, anything we notice gets recorded. And it's not unusual for one instructor to call another over to get a second perspective on a student's play. Although we often stop play and ask students about their game or choice of shot, we do not try to effect change.

When we finish our note taking, we send the students off for a snack and bed. Then the instructors and I go into conference.

Based on what we know about each player on and off the court, we try to form a quick description of his or her personality. To begin, we're simply looking for sketches, a way to identify the students who are going to be the most challenging.

The conferences goes on for a couple of hours. By the end of it, we hope to identify the students' major life issues (MLIs), personality traits that could explain the problems each student is having on (and off) the court. I'm always a little uncomfortable with the process: We meet a nice bunch of people and almost immediately begin studying their personal challenges. But right now we can still be objective, and we must be objective if we're going to help them.

Here are our initial evaluations of five of the students:*

● David, 22, a college senior whose overactive mind — so many choices — seems to slow his responses on and off the court.
● Diane, 29, an artist whose creativity may well be making her game inconsistent.
● Henry, 38, who owns a hardware store, whose strokes are very tight and who seems to be holding something in. (More than one of us suspect that something is anger.)
● Marla, 21, a college senior, who strikes us as a lot brighter than she acts. She's the spacey young woman who asked a question when I talked to her team.

* We'll be following the progress of these five students throughout the book.

● Marty, 17, a high school junior, who seems to be better at dreaming than working.

Finally, we call it a night. It's midnight, and a cup of tea before bed sounds great. We head to the dining room and find several students still up. Friendships form fast here.

Lesson 2

The second lesson — all the lessons — begins with the meditation exercise.

"It's important for your body to learn to recognize the breathing pattern that sets off the relaxation response. Over time, after practicing this meditation repeatedly, it will take only a few seconds of breathing this way to calm you down on the court or anywhere else. If you're playing and feel yourself getting angry or losing focus, close your eyes and think the breathing pattern, and you'll relax. Best yet, the response is almost immediate because your body will have come to associate the breathing pattern with relaxation. To make the association stick, you have to repeat the pattern many times. That's why we start each lesson with meditation here and why we encourage you to continue daily practice after you leave.

READER: **Please join in.**

"Everyone get comfortable and close your eyes. Again, breathe in one nostril and out the other, and then breathe in the same nostril and out the first. We're going to breathe for about eighteen minutes. Don't worry about the time. I'll let you know when to open your eyes."

The time passes quickly. "Okay, take a minute and then open your eyes. Is everyone back? Was that relaxing?"

A hand goes up. "What if I find myself thinking about stuff while I'm doing the breathing?"

"Good question. First, don't intentionally think about anything. Don't plan lunch. Don't make a list of the people you have to call. If a thought comes to you, just let it pass. Don't try to ignore it or get angry. Does that help?"

He nods and says, "I think that was about what I did. I just let the thoughts come and go."

"Any other questions?"

Everyone is looking at me expectantly. "Okay, it's time to focus on hitting the ball. I'm talking about the two or three seconds from the time your opponent strikes the ball until you hit it back. What are you thinking about during that time? Now don't confuse 'personality noise' — like, 'Oh no, another backhand' — with thinking. As soon as the ball is en route, somewhere in the back of your mind a part of your mind is thinking about your target, where you want the stroke you hit to go: 'deep in that corner,' 'sharp crosscourt,' even 'just get it back over the net.' The point of that thinking is to convey some idea of what you want your body to do.

"In the real world, of course, often thoughts don't get the job done. So what's a mind to do? The short answer: nothing. The zone state is mindless, or at least that's our experience of it. But the conscious mind is difficult to turn off. Want proof? Try sitting and not having any thoughts. Really. Starting now."

I pause here for about ten seconds. All of the students, their heads full of thoughts, are laughing.

"Most forms of meditation try to teach you to shut off your conscious mind. The process usually involves reducing the number of thoughts to one and then allowing that one thought to fall away, like when you forget the breathing technique. One way to stop yourself thinking is to give yourself a single distraction. Meditations use mantras and chants or breathing patterns — like the breathing pattern we use. You have to occupy your conscious mind on one thought during the stroke, or you will not zone.

"One thing, though: That thought has to have meaning. One famous consciousness-distraction technique encourages players to watch the spinning lines on the ball. What happens? In short order, your conscious mind becomes bored and you need a new distraction. To keep your conscious mind from filling your head with useless thoughts, you have to occupy it with something important.

"About now, some of you may be thinking, 'Well, when we meditate you tell us to focus on our breathing, and thoughts don't come much more meaningless than that.' And in a way, you're right. But meditation as we teach it here is a relaxation technique, a method you can call on to calm yourself, to catch your breath. And when you're meditating, you're not trying to carry out an actual task; you're just sitting there. However, when you fall into a zone state while you're working or playing music or reading, you have to be mentally focused — at least in part — on what you're doing. "The same applies to tennis: When you're on the court, you have to occupy your conscious mind in a productive way. That will keep your doubts, fears, and anxieties at bay. In plain English, if you fill your head with good thoughts, the bad ones won't have any room. And when you're executing a stroke, there's only one thing you should be thinking about: *What do I want this shot to do?*

"When Michael Jordan goes to the hoop, he's thinking about scoring, not each move he's making. The goal is never to make a good move; it's to score a basket. In tennis, the goal is never to make a good stroke; it's to hit a good shot. Good strokers lose to good players all the time.

"In those few seconds when you're preparing to hit the ball and then swinging, I want you to reduce your total 'thoughtload' by thinking one thought: *What do I want this shot to do?* Of course your ultimate goal — the conscious experience of a zone — is no thoughts. But for now, better one productive thought than all the unproductive ones you're probably having whenever you swing.

"I'm going to be talking about targeting; but notice that I want you to be thinking about what you want the shot to do, not just where you want it to go. By *target* here I mean something much more than a spot on the ground on the other side of the court. I mean the entirety of the shot you want to hit — spin, speed, height, everything.

Figure 3

Spot targeting

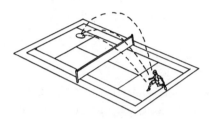

A target should define the shot
you want to hit.

"There are two good reasons why I don't recommend a spot on the other side of the court as a target.* The first is that a spot on the other side of the court does not define the shot you're hitting, only the endpoint. You can hit the same spot with a smash, a lob, a slice, a topspin, or a dozen other strokes (Figure 3). A location on the ground simply doesn't tell your body enough about what you want it to do.

"The second reason I don't suggest a target spot is that you can easily 'prethink it.' That means that you think about the target while you're running toward the ball, but that you're no longer focused on it at the moment you actually swing. After you swing, you probably think you had a good target . . . which you did, just not during the swing. For the target strategy to work, you have to be thinking about the target while you're executing the swing.

"We've all had days when we aren't watching the ball well. You know, you begin saying over and over to yourself, 'Watch the ball. Watch the ball.' What happens? On the very next ball, you don't watch. That tells us that there's no guarantee that thinking about a shot before you swing is going to do you a bit of good while you're swinging. The same is true of a target: You must be thinking about it at the moment you swing.

"What do I mean, then, when I talk about a target? In part, your tar-

* Many coaches encourage their players to target a certain height over the net.
  That strategy shares the same drawbacks as targeting a certain spot on the court.

LESSON 2

get is the trajectory of the shot you want to hit. By choosing a trajectory, you define the shot for your body. The trajectory tells your body not only where you want the ball to land on the other side of the court, but also the height and pace and spin you want on your return. Your body uses that information to get you where you need to be and to execute the shot. Notice that all you have to do is focus on the trajectory: Your body takes care of the rest instinctively, without conscious input from you.

"At the end of Lesson 1, I talked about animals and how they perform in the absence of conscious thought. That's the kind of instinctive performance you should be having on the court. Conscious thought is necessary for just two things in tennis and other sports. The first is motivation. Tennis skills are not survival skills: If you lose a match, you still go home and have supper; you won't *be* supper. We usually assume that players are properly motivated, but that isn't always the case. Sometimes aspects of a player's personality lead to failure. Notice that I said *properly motivated*. I'm not talking about wanting to win; I'm talking about not shooting yourself in the foot, not letting elements of your personality prevent you from succeeding. We talk more about this in Lesson 4.

"Conscious thought is also necessary to define goals based on the rules and strategies of tennis. It's possible that people have been running around with clubs and other racketlike objects for thousands of years, but the rules and strategies of the game are not innate. This second task of the conscious mind, defining your goals, is our topic today. That's the role of targeting.

"Here's how it works. As soon as your opponent hits the ball, you begin thinking about the shot *you* plan to hit: where and how you want the ball to land on the other side of the court.

"From the instant the ball leaves your opponent's racket, you have a sense of where the ball is going to land on your side of the court, but your focus is on the trajectory of the shot you're going to make. That's the decision that defines your goals, that tells your body what it has to do. Once you've established the trajectory of your shot, your focus shifts to the flight of the ball coming toward you and the point where that trajectory will intersect with the outgoing trajectory — the point of impact.

"At The Zone, when we talk about targeting, we talk about seeing a *V*. In the abstract, what you visualize when you're deciding on your shot looks like a *V*: two intersecting lines — the outgoing and incoming trajectories — that meet at the point of impact. In reality, of course, the trajectories are seldom straight, like the lines that form a *V*; instead they curve somewhat and form a less-than-perfect *V*.

"As you run toward the ball, you begin to envision the trajectory of the shot you're going to hit; you actually see a line in the air.* At the same time, out of the corner of your eye, you're looking at the ball and the trajectory it's following as it comes toward you. Notice that you're looking at

* Sometimes, I see two different trajectories (lines), but I almost immediately decide on one. More on that below.

41   LESSON 2

Figure 4
Shifting trajectories

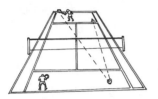

a. The V, the anticipated trajectory

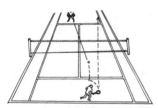

b. The less-than-perfect *V*

the ball; you're not mesmerized by it. Watching the ball should never be a task unto itself. The point of watching the ball is to update the information you're gathering about the impact point and the stroke you're going to hit.

"Again, the *V* isn't a 'perfect' *V*. It's two curved lines. More often than not, as you run toward the ball, the outgoing trajectory — the line of the shot you're planning to make — shifts in the air (Figure 4). Why? In part because you're seeing it from different angles as you're moving and in part because your approximate impact point grows more accurate as the ball approaches.

"The actual point of impact, however, is always an approximation. That's because you must begin your swing before the ball actually reaches the impact point. Have you ever seen small children reach for a moving object and miss it? It happens because they reach for the spot where the object was when they gave the mental command to grab it. In the same way, if you wait to begin your swing until the ball is at the impact point, you're never going to hit the ball. Because you have to swing before the ball reaches the impact point, you have to project the last few feet of the ball's flight toward you. At The Zone, we ask you to see that projection as a line in the air, and that line is the second part of the *V*.

"At this point, as I begin to swing, my *V* becomes just a small piece, just a couple of feet, of the incoming and outgoing trajectories, and the intersection of those two lines, the spot where I expect to hit the ball (Figure 5).

Figure 5
The final *V*

"Why envision a *V* instead of a simple line outward? Because it's too easy to prethink a trajectory and then not think about it at the instant you swing. To see a *V*, you have to be focused in the moment you're hitting the ball. Why? Because one line of the *V*, the incoming shot, starts with the ball itself, and that ball is absolutely in the moment.

"Remember, the flight paths must include everything: height, spin, destination, and speed. It shouldn't just be a flat line. Also, the last few feet of the shot coming in will approach you from all different directions. Make your *V* reflect this. Short hops come sharply up from the ground, and overheads fall from the sky. Sometimes a *V* is an oversimplification. It moves in different positions and the lines are usually curved, and one can be on top of the other, but they're something like a *V* (Figure 6).

"Other things to remember: You must define a new target for each stroke. Don't run over to a ball and think, 'I want to hit this one just like I hit the last one.' I've seen players, particularly juniors drilling, who look as though they're set on autopilot. They aren't thinking at all; they're just repeating whatever stroke the drill requires. But tennis isn't a drill. Every stroke should be a response to a unique set of circumstances.

"How do you choose a shot? The decision rests on many elements. Where is your opponent now, and where is he or she headed? What are your strengths? Which strokes come easily to you? What are your opponent's weaknesses? What is the match situation? These are just some of the factors you have to incorporate into choosing a good goal, a good *tar-*

Figure 6
A variety of Vs

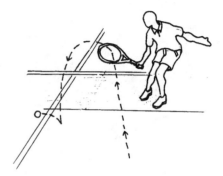

a. Groundstroke in, groundstroke out.

b. Groundstroke in, lob out.

c. Lob in, overhead smash out.

d. Passing shot in, drop shot out.

get, for each shot. And you get just a couple of seconds to do it. That's the bad news. The good news is you all can do it.

"I noted earlier that I often see two possible outward trajectories when a ball is hit toward me. For example, I might see a passing shot and a lob almost at once. That's fine as long as I make a quick choice between them. A quick decision is key to the process. You must have one clear shot in mind when you swing, and you want to give your body as much time as possible to construct a shot. If you routinely have trouble choosing between two possible shots, you must work on decisiveness. And once you've made a decision, stick with it. Don't change your mind during the execution.

"Another don't: Don't waste mental effort tracking the ball. Your eyes will track the ball automatically; eyes are drawn naturally to moving objects. Early in the flight of the ball toward you, your perceptual task is simple. While the ball is still a good distance from you, it's very easy to keep tabs on it. This is the time, then, when you want to be using your mind to construct your return shot. Later, as the ball nears the point of impact, the perceptual task gets harder (more later) and your focus needs to shift back to the ball.

"Although your opponent controls the trajectory of the ball coming toward you, generally you control the point of impact — you decide where along the trajectory you're going to hit the ball. On most strokes, you have a wide number of choices. At work are three factors: the shot you want to create, the flight of the ball coming toward you, and the position of your racket. Assuming you've already visualized both the shot you plan to make and the trajectory of the ball flying toward you, you want to optimize the way you use your racket. My advice is to see your Vs as far in front of your body as possible, to hit the ball as early as you can, at a height with which you're comfortable."

"When I talk about hitting the ball early, I'm talking about hitting the ball as far forward as possible. And by *forward*, I mean in front of your body. The primary reason: People are designed to see forward, so that's where a tennis ball is meant to be hit. When Andre Agassi is 'on,' for example, he hits very far forward and very accurately. When he's 'off,' he's just a little late. Of course his new impact point necessitates a head movement, and he doesn't have the same accuracy.

"Can I get a volunteer?"

A young man stands up and comes forward. I position him about ten feet from me, say "Catch," and toss him a tennis ball.

He catches the ball in front of him.

"Did you notice where you caught the ball?" I ask.

"Well, I reached forward, I guess."

I nod and say, "As most people do. We're designed to respond to activity in front of us."

I hand the student a tennis racket. "One more demonstration, please. Take this racket and pretend it's a club and I'm a wild animal. How would you defend yourself against me?"

As I make a move toward him, he swings the racket out well in front of his body.

"Good. Do you see that if you were defending yourself from something coming at you, you would block it in front of you. And if you were striking at prey, you would strike it in front of you. It's easier to see something that's in front of you, and that speaks to the efficiency, the accuracy, even the power with which you hit the ball.

"Of course, sometimes you can't hit the ball early, but you can still hit it well. The other day I was running down a forehand deep and wide that already was past me. I could see the impact point, my *V*, hanging in the air. All I had to do was reach for it. I don't think I could reproduce or even describe that stroke for all the tea in China, but I had my impact point to work with. As long as you see the *V*, you have a shot.

"Another point. Suppose you're visualizing a *V*, and it changes. Say the ball takes a bad bounce or you misjudged its speed, and you find yourself out of position to take the crosscourt stroke you'd been planning. What now? Your nonconscious will make an almost-instantaneous correction to a shot that is possible. It may not be a great shot, but it will be the best you can do.

"What's key at a moment like this is not to lose focus. You must trust your body to do its thing. Conscious corrections are slow. Just let the non-conscious correction happen. I honestly believe that sometimes my non-conscious intentionally mis-hits the ball to produce whatever shot I'm envisioning. On many occasions I've hit shots to the exact spot I intended by a combination of bad bounce, strange swing, racket-face twist, and off-center hit on the racket. I'm always amazed when it happens. It's as though as soon as the ball bounces bad, my nonconscious calculates that by opening up the racket face and hitting the ball off the strings near the frame, it can produce a shot almost like the one I was envisioning before the ball bounced bad. I know. You're thinking, 'That's just a lucky shot.' But I've hit too many of those shots to believe that they're accidents. Of course, we all hit accidental winners; but when you're really focused, there seems to be more purpose in all your shots.

"I know what I've been talking about — envisioning all of these lines while the ball is traveling toward you — sounds like a lot to do. In reality, the most difficult part of the process is choosing a target quickly. Almost as soon as the ball leaves your opponent's racket, you should be finalizing a target and begin creating your *V*. It's not impossible to create a *V* near the end of the ball's flight toward you, but there is a calm and a consistency that come with defining the trajectories early, when it takes less effort to watch the ball.

"One more thing. Sometimes you do everything right, but the shot misses. When that happens to me, I stop at the spot and create a new trajectory, as though to say to my nonconscious, 'Next time a little higher' or 'Next time more spin.' It's just a gentle correction to myself. I picture the *V* I want to hit; and the next time I need the shot, I have a memory of where to find it.

"Okay, now, out to the courts."

Session 2

We begin by having everyone stretch and warm up. Then we pair the students up and ask them as they rally to feel where the impact point of each shot is in relation to their head. After a few minutes, we move onto the courts to help them adjust their impact points. When they're feeling comfortable with swinging in front of their bodies, we ask them to try to see a *V* with every stroke and to call out a score with each shot. We use the 0 to 3 rating system: Here, a 0 means no *V* at all; a 1 means the player at least thought about a target; a 2 is some sort of target; and a 3 is a *V*. We track scores and strokes. We want to know which strokes produce the lowest scores.

"Remember," I tell one student who's clearly having a problem seeing the *V*s, "to be effective, the target must be in your head at the moment you swing. That's why we use the ball's flight toward you as one line in the *V*. The flight of the ball is very in the moment."

After we've watched the play on each court, I call the students over. "One more piece of advice," I say. "Don't scold yourself when you don't see

Figure 7
Target practice

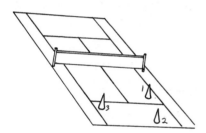

a *V*. Just notice the strokes with which you have a problem seeing a *V* or the times the *V* doesn't work. Maybe you're having trouble on all short balls or overheads. Or maybe the trouble you're having is situation-specific, in matches or tiebreakers, for example. Just notice and keep trying to form your targets."

While I'm talking, the other instructors are setting up cones on two of the courts. They spread them out — three to a court — so there won't be any accidental "winners." The cones on each court are numbered 1 through 3 (Figure 7).

We ask four students to line up at each court, facing the cones across the net. An instructor feeds a ball to each student in turn, calling out the number of the target cone. The student hits one shot, aiming for the target, and then goes to the back of the line. We give 3 points for a direct hit, 2 points for a one-bounce hit, and 1 point for a very near miss.

In this and other drills of this type, about a third of the time — and sometimes for several shots in row — the instructors do not call out a target number. Instead the students must choose a target and call it out themselves as they're swinging. On all tries we deduct a point for "shots nowhere" — shots that totally miss the target.

I explain the drill to the students and finish up saying, "Trying to hit with this level of accuracy may be new to some of you. It takes time to get used to the *V*, but the targets should help. Eventually you'll have to make your own targets, but all in good time."

We spend a lot of time at The Zone working on Vs, a schedule that reflects the importance of targeting shots in tennis. I've found that just an awareness of Vs can improve play significantly, especially many of the borderline strokes, the not-too-bad-but-not-so-great ones. Creating a target is also an excellent way to recover a game that's gone astray, particularly when one of a player's good strokes goes haywire.

After a half an hour or so of target practice, I talk to the group again. I start with the role the V can play in improving mediocre strokes and recovering good ones. Then I go on: "Seeing the V has an added benefit: While you're focusing on a V, you can't be focusing on the stuff you usually think about when you come up against one of your problem strokes. You know, the 'Uh-oh, another backhand' kind of stuff. Of course, at first, all that old noise that always goes off in your head will be resisting the V, and you'll forget to look for it or to focus on it. That noise is simply incompatible with the V. But on some strokes, the V is going to win. When it does, you may actually feel that something is missing or that something is different. It is: You're functioning without the old negative thoughts.

"And what functioning! You might swing with a very clear target on one particular stroke and immediately notice how loose the swing felt, how easily the stroke happened, or how calm and focused you were. In an instant, you realize how tight you've been, how scared or nervous, or how unfocused. When that happens, make sure you write down your thoughts

READER: If you're a coach who would like to add more thought drills to your collection, try the three described below. If you're a player, find a hitting partner and go out and try one. I think you'll find the drills very helpful.

and feelings: 'My stroke shifted.' 'I hit the ball earlier.' 'My feet felt steadier.' Write down something to help you remember the sensation."

We spend the rest of the session doing drills. Once we've identified problem strokes in Session 1, we seldom ask students to hit a specific stroke: We want them thinking about targeting, not working on stroke production. Because these aren't the usual drills ("Hit crosscourt forehands"), they need some explaining; and because they're challenging, some students — especially the juniors — don't like them at first. In short order, though, they find the drills interesting to do and appreciate the practice on all aspects of their game, strengths and weaknesses. We tell them that it's more important to practice their weaknesses than their strengths, even if they don't like doing so . . . *especially* if they don't like doing so.

Drill 1: Target practice

Players: Two to a court.

Preparing the court: On one side, using tape, outline two triangular targets on the diagonal that cuts across the service boxes from the center strap on the net to the outside corners of the court (Figure 8).

How it works: The play begins. Player 1 (the player on the opposite side of the net from the targets) must try to hit one of the targets within five

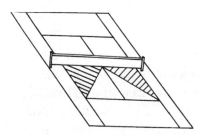

Figure 8
Drill 1

strokes; if not, Player 2 wins a point. If Player 1 hits one of the targets, Player 2 has one stroke to return the shot and hit a winner. If Player 2 does not hit a winner on the very next stroke, Player 1 earns 2 points. This is the only way Player 1 can score points. Player 2 wins 1 point every time he or she either wins a rally or prevents Player 1 from hitting a target zone within five strokes. Players switch sides every ten minutes or after one player wins 10 points.

Variations: The drill can be played with or without allowing Player 1 to come to the net. If Player 1 does not hit the target in the first four strokes, he or she must try to hit it on the last stroke.

Lessons learned: This drill teaches Player 1 to plan a strategy, to hit drop shots and at sharp angles, and to visualize targets. For Player 2, it offers practice hitting deep defensively (to prevent Player 1 from getting off sharp-angled shots). Also, Player 2 must be prepared to go on the offensive each time Player 1 hits a target zone. NOTE: If Player 2 begins to lose rallies on purpose — remember, no points are scored when Player 2 loses a rally, Player 1 should get a new practice partner.

Drill 2: Lobs and overheads

Players: Two to a court.

How it works: Player 1 starts at the service line; Player 2, at the baseline on the other side of the court. Player 1 hits the ball into play. Player 2 must return a lob, calling out a target zone — "Crosscourt" or "Down the line" — as he or she swings. Player 1 must return an overhead shot. If the overhead misses the target zone, Player 2 gets a point. If Player 1 hits the target zone, Player 2 must return a lob, again calling out a target zone. Play continues until Player 1 misses the target zone or Player 2 fails to return a lob. Player 2 can choose not to call out a target zone, and the players simply play out the point. Whoever wins the point gets 1 point.

In each rally, Player 2 can call out a target zone three times (this number can be changed depending on the players' skill level); after that, the overhead hitter is free to try to win the point. The object here is for Player 2 to hit a good lob and then *not* call out a target zone, which maximizes his or her chance of winning the point. Player 1 must stay ready to choose a stroke and a target zone whenever Player 2 fails to call out a target. If Player 2 fails to get an overhead back, he or she loses the point. Players switch sides every ten minutes or after one player wins 10 points.

Lessons learned: Player 1 and 2 both learn patience. Player 2 learns the value of a well-placed lob. (The object is really to call targets on weak lobs and not call them on good lobs because Player 1 is more likely to win the point.) Player 2 learns to play angles on overheads and to make decisions (whenever Player 1 chooses not to call a target).

Drill 3: Dink drill

Players: Two to a court.

How it works: Player 1 stands a few steps behind the service line (farther back for better players); Player 2 stands on the opposite baseline. Player 1 hits a start-the-point approach shot to Player 2, who hits a soft return, no lobs or passing shots. Player 1 must hit a winner on the very next stroke or Player 2 gets 1 point. Players switch sides every ten minutes or after one player wins 10 points.

Lessons learned: The drill gives Player 1 practice in targeting approach shots to set up winners, finishing off easy ones, and dealing intelligently with dinks. It gives Player 2 practice in hitting dinks and in deciding what to do next — often a good dink elicits a drop shot in return — and doing it quickly. It also gives Player 2 practice in reading opponents and guessing where to run.

●

Before we send the students off, I speak to them again: "Remember that part of seeing the *V* is choosing your stroke. Choosing challenging strokes helps to keep your interest and to improve your play. Your body likes the challenge. Unless you're desperate, you should never be thinking, 'I just have to get the ball back.'

"Another thing. At the beginning, you're not going to see a *V* on every shot. It may be a while — a long while — before you get the feel for it. But it should begin to happen often enough for you to tell that when you're able to create a clear *V*, your performance is very good.*

"Know, too, that long after you begin using *V*s, you'll sometimes forget. Why? It's human nature. People often repeat behavior that produces a negative result: a bad relationship, unhappiness with a job, a hassle. That tendency is one of the ways we shoot ourselves in the foot. And until we're living in a more enlightened state, we're going to continue to do things that keep us from our goals.

"When you're watching the ball approach, a pattern of thoughts or feelings is running through your head. That's what's keeping you from making a *V* much of the time. You simply have too much other stuff going on . . . consciously or not. You need to get your mind fully occupied by your *V*. Work at it a little. Don't give up. I assure you that this type of targeting can only help your game and you."

* Very high level players might choose to use *V*s on selected strokes if they feel they target some strokes well already. Most players should use them on every stroke.

Lesson 3

READER: **Please do the same.**

We begin with a meditation. Everyone has come to expect it and to enjoy the break from the day.

"Get comfortable and close your eyes. Let's do our breathing for about eighteen minutes."

"Now take a minute and then open your eyes. Everyone back?"

I wait a moment and then say, "Okay, we're going to take the *V* a step further. I want you to remember that the point of the *V*, where the lines meet, defines your *impact point*, the spot where you want your racket to connect with the ball. This is crucial. That point gives your eyes a focal point.

"You must define your impact point before you swing. Here's why. I want each of you to put a hand up in front of your face and shake your head. What do you see?"

A couple of students are laughing as they swing their heads first right and then left.

"Not much, eh? Your vision while your head is moving is pretty poor. In those final milliseconds, when they're uncorking their swing, most players fight to keep their eyes glued to the ball. But most of that is a waste of time.

"Now try the experiment with your hand in front of your face again. This time, move your head back and forth *and* shake your hand. Your vision is almost nil.

"Let's put these facts together. As the ball is flying toward you, you're watching it, your head near motionless for most of its flight. You've already seen how when you look at an object that is far away and coming at you, like a ball, your eyes can follow the object for long distances without your turning your head. But somewhere between the bounce of the ball and the impact point, you jerk your neck and head around as you try to watch the ball. Don't bother. Your vision is so poor with your head jerking around that it's almost impossible to see a rapidly-moving ball.

READER: **You too.**

"Everyone try this. Pick two areas or objects in the room, two corners or two pictures, for example. The areas or objects must be far enough away from each other so that looking from one to the other forces you to turn your head ninety degrees. Now, look at one and then turn your head quickly to the other, back and forth. Do this a few times, and then ask yourself two questions: How quickly did the two areas or objects come into clear view? And were you able to see anything in between the two objects? My guess is that you see the two areas or objects almost immediately and that you see almost nothing in between them.

"If your impact point is not far enough out in front of your body, then at some point, as the ball gets close, you must begin using your head and neck to follow the ball. Lo and behold, unless the ball is moving very slowly, which we'll talk about in a bit, you can't see it. But you can still see the impact of the racket on the ball.

"The two-object demonstration shows us that the only way you can move your head and still see clearly is if you know in advance where your eyes are headed and what they're looking for. That's why seeing the *V* is so critical. If you know the impact point — that is, if you have the *V* in your mind's eye — then you have a visual image to turn your head toward and so a good chance of seeing the impact.

"Again, to create a focal point at the point of impact, you must see the *V* well before you move your head. Then, wherever the impact point turns out to be, you know where to move your eyes and will be able to see your racket connect with the ball.

"What I'm about to say is very different from what you've been told since you first picked up a racket. Yes, you should be watching the ball as it comes toward you. But when the ball nears the impact point, *stop looking at it*. At that moment, the ball should not be your primary focus. Oh, you'll see it — the ball never leaves your field of vision — but it's not your focal point. What is? The point of the *V*, the impact point you've been planning since the ball left your opponent's racket.

"Stop watching the ball. A radical thought, yes? Not really. In fact, most players must take their eyes off the ball to see the point of impact. A player who doesn't is going to jerk his or her head and not see the ball anyway."

I pause and then sum up: "So here is the experience, all happening in a couple of milliseconds: The ball is a few feet in front of you. If you haven't hit it yet, you're forced to move your head to keep watching it. At that point you should be rushing your eyes to the impact point. Let the ball go. Remember that if you can form your *V* in front of you, you won't have to jerk your head to see the impact. Of course, that isn't always possible, even for very good players.

"A question: Why do you track the tennis ball?"

I didn't expect it, but I get an answer.

"Because you want to hit it."

"That's right. Your main objective for watching the ball is to help you hit it. Once you've projected your impact point, the ball has served its purpose. Suppose you were hitting tennis balls in a room, and I could make the room pitch-black at any moment. Do you think the lights going out when the ball is a foot from impact would affect your swing or the shot? Absolutely not. You've already begun your swing, and there's little you can do to change it.

"Well, if that's true, why do you need to be looking at the ball when it's a foot away? You've already created the impact point somewhere in your head and unleashed your swing. The ball is almost superfluous: Now, the impact point is everything.

"So when should you know where the impact point is going to be?"

Another student responds: "I think it would depend on how hard the ball was hit."

"That's part of it. I think we can all agree that the accuracy of the impact point increases as the ball comes closer. You start with a guess — we all do — and then continuously adjust the impact point as the ball moves toward you. Have you ever noticed how easy it is to return a hard-hit ground stroke that lands short, say near the service line? That's because you've got plenty of time to project its impact point. On the other hand, it's a lot harder to return a ball that's been hit softly and loopy and lands deep, near the baseline, because you have so little time after the bounce to project an impact point (Figure 9).

"The second at which you can move your eyes from the ball varies, and only you can know when it is. You'll be picturing a *V*, adjusting it as the ball comes toward you, and at some point the *V* becomes 'believable.' Suddenly you sense that the ball is headed there and that it's time to make that impact point come true. It's a feeling.

"How do you develop the head-jerking behavior in the first place? When you're first learning and receiving softly hit, loopy balls, the head-jerking behavior works. You can see the ball all the way to the racket by tracking it with your eyes and head, so many players do that without thinking. But when their skill improves and their opponents hit harder, when the ball is moving fast, they find they can't track it with their heads. Unhappily, by that time it's already a habit."

Figure 9
Incoming trajectories

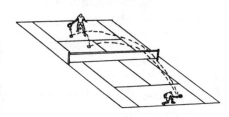

LESSON 3

A student calls out: "If you can't change your swing when the ball is close, why do you need to see the impact at all?"

"Great question. I'm going to give you just part of the answer right now; the rest will come in time. It's about learning. In tennis there's no better feedback than watching the racket connect with the ball. The information you glean from the impact — how the ball hits the strings and how and where it flies — is processed by your nonconscious mind and is crucial to perfecting your technique. It's almost like watching a videotape of your performance with the added benefit of immediacy: You see it as it happens. Feedback is most effective when it's instantaneous.

"I should say that some players can see the impact of racket and ball without focusing on the impact point. They're like people who can wiggle their ears. Either they naturally prefer to connect with the ball at a point well in front of themselves, which requires very little head turning, or they have a special knack for tracking visual objects. Those are gifts but not necessities. The technique you're learning here is for the ninety-five percent of players who rarely if ever see the racket hit the ball."

I stop and ask for a volunteer. Lots of hands go up. I pick Dale, a woman sitting near the front of the group.

"I'm going to put a penny down on the floor and drop a tennis ball on top of it. I want you to watch and tell me if I hit the penny. Okay?"

She nods yes. I place the penny on the floor and get ready to drop a ball from about three feet directly over the penny.

"Are you ready?"

Dale nods again.

"Okay, now don't move at all. Stay absolutely still. Where are you looking?"

She, of course, is staring at the penny.

"Why aren't you going to try to track the ball down to the penny?"

Dale laughs as she realizes the point of the demonstration. "I didn't even think about watching the ball fall. It just seems that if you want to see the ball hit the penny, you should watch the penny because the penny isn't moving."

"And the impact point isn't moving either," I say. "Did you ever notice that the linespeople at a tennis match stare at the line and wait for the ball to come into view? They don't track the ball to see its impact with the ground. They know approximately where the impact is going to be, and they watch that area. By creating a clear impact point, you too have a fixed object to look at, which gives you a better view of the ball hitting the racket.

"Remember, during the stroke, the ball never really falls from your field of vision. Yes, your focus shifts to the impact point as the ball travels the last few feet — at most — toward you, but the ball is always within your sight. And a split second later, as the ball reaches the point of impact, it's again part of your focal point. In the interim, your vision has steadied on the impact point, so that when the ball reaches that point it's plainly visible.

"I can't describe the feeling. It's very in the moment. Your conscious mind is steadied by the clarity of the impact, the ball and the strings, while your body is freely engaged in producing the stroke. When you look up a second later and see the ball flying toward its target, it's magic.

"Again, there's no precise point at which you should change your focus. I can tell you only that it should happen at the instant you're convinced that your *V* is accurate. On short but firmly hit balls to you, you may jump to the impact point when the ball is still five feet away. On a heavy top-spinning deep shot, the shift may come when the ball is less than a foot away. On a volley shot, you may have to finalize your *V* and then jump to the impact point immediately after your opponent hits the ball. When I used to watch the great Boris Becker dive for a ball, I was certain he was doing just that, that he'd already seen the impact point and his body was simply making it happen.

"I remember going to a party once where a group of people decided to hold a Ping-Pong tournament. I hadn't played seriously in twenty years, but I had been pretty good. As it turned out, the tournament ran long, and I had to leave before it ended, but I had made it to the finals. I was on my way out as my two possible opponents began their match, when a man stopped me and said, 'You were going to win, weren't you?' 'I think so,' I said, 'but why do *you* think so?' 'I saw the way you watched the ball,' he answered.

"It was very perceptive of him. I hadn't played Ping-Pong since I began playing New Age tennis myself, so the experience was new to me. I obviously didn't feel very practiced that night — it had been many years since I played — but I had a clarity watching the ball that I had never had when I first played the game.

"So much of what you learn here about focusing on the impact point can be transferred to other sports: The baseball *V*, for example, is very like the tennis *V*: The pitch is the shot coming toward you; the hit is the shot you're making. Here, too, players do better when they hit the ball in front of themselves, when they almost leap the last few feet to the impact point. In golf, the trajectory of the projected shot is one stroke of the *V*, and the follow-through with the head of the club is the other.

"Now, two things to remember: First, only the targets you visualize at the time of the stroke count here. Early targets are better than none, but in terms of occupying your conscious mind, the moment you swing is crucial. Besides, what other conscious thought could you possibly want in your head at the moment you swing? Your zone state will produce the swing mindlessly, easily, enjoyably. Second, there will be times when you can't or just don't visualize the impact point. When that happens, go easy on yourself!

"So, let's get out on the courts and see if we can take the *V* one step further, to prepare you for the instant when racket and ball connect."

Session 3

"I have an exercise that will help you see where you should be striking the ball. I need a volunteer."

I get one, Marty.

"Stand at the baseline, and hold your racket as though you're going to hit a forehand ground stroke."

He does. One of the instructors, Dan, takes a ball and stands on the baseline on the opposite side of the net.

"Dan is going to pretend that he's holding a struck ball [*Dan walks forward.*] that's flying toward Marty. Then [*Dan climbs over the net.*] the ball sails maybe a foot or two over the net and lands [*Dan bends to the ground.*] a few feet behind the service line, and then bounces up to a height of three or four feet and flies toward Marty [*Dan stops.*]."

Marty is pretending he's watching a real ball coming at him.

"Notice that Marty has watched the ball approach all the way from the other side of the court, bounce, and come within a few feet of him without ever moving his head. He's doing all of the tracking with his eyes — and a few minor adjustments of other parts of his body. Now, however, as the ball moves to within a few feet of Marty [*Dan gets closer to Marty.*], he has to jerk his head around to try to see the ball whizzing by.

"Did you all see when Marty's head jerked? By the time he was forced to turn his head, he should have started to swing at the ball. That's what we're going to practice first today: choosing an impact point in front of your body."

We begin the practice with an exercise to help the students form and focus on their *V*s. We break them up into small groups and walk with each group around a court. We want them to picture (and practice) different strokes and to envision a number of different *V*s. I explain the process and say, "If we skip a stroke that you hit frequently or have a question about, please tell us. Others probably want to practice the stroke too."

This exercise can begin anywhere on the court. We start at the net, approximately where the player volleys from.

I say to my group, "I want you to 'see' the different *V*s that go with a high forehand, a low forehand, both crosscourt and up the line, deep replies, and drop shots. Mentally practice whatever shot you imagine, and envision the *V*s. Do each shot at least five times."

As the students stand at the net, I call out each forehand shot in turn. Their task: to see the *V,* to imagine that a ball is flying toward them and then that they are hitting the ball toward their target. I allow a few minutes for each stroke and then call out another.

After the students finish their forehand *V*s at the net, I have them do backhand volleys in all their variations. Finally, to reinforce the students' mental images, I have them stand at the net and hit volleys back and forth for several minutes.

Table 1
Picture practice

Players' location on the court	Practice shots
Net	High forehand, low forehand crosscourt, low forehand up the line, deep replies, drop shots
Midcourt	Approach shots, put-aways, short hops, drop shots, overheads
Baseline	Ground strokes, service, service returns

When they've finished at the net, we move to the midcourt and practice — first mentally and then physically — the *V*s that go with midcourt shots, approaches, put-aways, short hops, drop shots, and the like (Table 1). Then we move on to the baseline. This exercise is one we repeat over several sessions. It's been shown that mental practice is an effective way to help learn a motor skill.

When all the groups have finished, I share a few pointers: "Whenever you're practicing and you experience a shot that you feel you didn't target clearly because you weren't sure what to play, go to the spot and envision at least one shot and the *V* it forms. Then mentally practice the shot — and the *V* that goes with it — a few times.

"I believe mental practice works best when you do two things: First, live each shot. You want to be experiencing the shot as though it's happening. See the ball flying toward you, form your *V*, even swing your racket where you envision the impact point to be. Don't do mental practice as though you're watching TV. Even if you're sitting down at the kitchen table, you should see it as though you're on the court, not watching yourself like a spectator. Make it feel real.

"Second, experience the mental practice in real time. If you're actually using your racket on the court, picture your opponent hitting a hot passing shot up the line, immediately form a crosscourt *V*, and move to intercept the ball. Feel the shot in real time, and that feeling will stimulate a memory for your body to use when the shot actually happens."

The hitting practice in this session focuses on the impact point. Before the students start the drills, I remind them about shifting their focus as they're about to hit the ball: "Remember, don't get mesmerized by the ball. Watch it to create your impact point; but once you're sure of the impact point, that's where you should be looking. Also, rapid decision making is crucial. As soon as your opponent hits the ball, you want to choose your shot. And once you've formed a *V*, stay with it."

Drill 4: Focused ground strokes

Players: Two to a court.

How it works: The players begin at the baselines, each to the right of but near the centerline, and try to hit crosscourt to where their opponent is standing. With each successive crosscourt shot, the players must target an area a little closer to the sideline than the last shot they hit. The first player who hits a ball out of bounds or back toward the centerline loses the point. When a player misses a shot — that is, fails to place a shot nearer the sideline than his or her previous shot — the other player can hit the ball one more time and try to get closer to the sideline. If it works, that player gets a second point and the rally ends. A new rally begins at the centerline. The players should practice each stroke for ten minutes.

Variation: The players start at the centerline and try to hit closer and closer to the sideline. All the same rules apply. The only difference: This drill is down the line.

Drill 5: Precision passing shot

Players: Two to a court.

How it works: Player 1 hits an approach shot from the service line and then takes a position at the net. Player 2, standing at the baseline on the other side of the court, must return the shot — no lobbing. Player 1 must stand within two feet of the centerline (we're loose with this) until the passing shot is struck — a rule that leaves Player 2 with at least one good option. After ten minutes, the players should switch roles.

Drill 6: Precision deep lob

Players: Two to a court.

How it works: Player 1 stands at the service line and hits the ball to Player 2 at the baseline, who throws up a lob. All lobs must be hit high (or the player loses the point) and must be allowed to bounce. Lobs that land inside the service boxes automatically lose; lobs that land within two feet of the baseline automatically win. (This distance can be changed to suit the players' skill level or even to balance out a mismatched pair of players.) All other lobs are in play, and a point begins. After ten minutes, the players should switch roles.

Drills 4, 5, and 6 teach the students to be precise about the placement of their shots. They also encourage the students to concentrate: In these drills, it takes just one bad shot to lose the point.

Special Lesson/Session

To help students form *V*s more easily and to keep their frustration to a minimum, we teach a special lesson/session as soon as possible after we teach the *V*. The whole lesson/session is done on the courts.

"In the English language, we have many words for the vision function. We *look at,* we *watch,* we *perceive,* we *stare,* we *glare,* we *gaze,* we *peek,* we *view*. When asked what we do with our eyes, though, usually we use the word *see*. That same word, *see*, also is used to mean 'have understanding,' as in 'Oh, I see now.'

"Try this: I want you to stand in the middle of a court and choose two trees or fence posts that are less than ninety degrees apart. Face straight ahead, looking right in the middle of the space between the two objects, and look from one to the other to see if the trees or fence posts are exactly the same color. Look back and forth several times to be sure.

"Now try this: Pretend that there's a person standing in front of each tree or fence post, and you think one of them is a liar. The two people are talking with each other, so you take this opportunity to check them out.

Face straight ahead, looking right in the middle of the space between the two people, and look from one to the other to size them up. Look back and forth several times.

"What happens? If you're like most people, when you looked at the trees, you turned your head back and forth to see; and when you checked out the people, you probably moved your eyes more than your head. In other words, there are different ways of looking at things depending on what you want to do in your head with the visual input.

"If you want to *see* an object, to take in information about that object, you'll tend to keep the object in the center of your visual field, moving your head if necessary to do so. But if you're simply looking at an object with the idea of doing mental processing — remembering, planning, creating — you'll let your eyes shift off center . . . you won't move your head.

READER: **You try this too.**

"Try this: Look straight ahead. Now picture the face of an old friend. Take ten seconds to make the face as clear as you can." I count slowly and quietly to ten. "Okay. I bet your eyes moved, that they wandered to one side."

Several students nod.

"And I bet you're wondering why. The answer is simple: Just like there are different words for describing seeing, there are different ways of seeing. The key is why you're looking. The middle of your visual field is reserved for input. You watch TV straight on; you watch a movie straight on; you even watch a tennis match straight on, your head bouncing back

SPECIAL LESSON/SESSION

and forth to follow the action. But once you know what you need to know and are ready to begin processing that information, you don't need to be looking at it straight on.

"My point: When you're playing tennis, you rarely watch the ball straight on. When your eyes are fixed on center, your mind is focused on processing input. To free your mind to carry out other tasks — choosing a shot from a catalog of shots, for example — you have to move your eyes off center.

"Of course, you need to keep the ball in your field of vision, but you don't have to look at it head on. Watch it from the sides or corners of your eyes so your mind can stay active. The trick is to keep your head farther down than you probably are accustomed to doing. Because the ball is approaching on either your forehand or your backhand side, you're going to turn to that side. So now you're facing down and sideways. In that position, your eyes will be looking at the ball flying toward you from the top and sides, and that's perfect. That view should activate the portion of your brain that creates visual images, which is going to help you create your Vs."

I move to the baseline of one of the courts. "Look at my stance. The ball is coming toward me, heading exactly where I'm staring, down and to the side. As it approaches, I'm forming and then adjusting my V. The processing done — I've seen my V — I focus on the impact point, which is *exactly where my head has been facing all along*. For that final millisecond, with the ball straight in front of me, I watch it hit the strings of my racket.

"At the instant of impact, when the ball is right in front of you, your brain is primed for input, and you need to be watching. When you hit that ball, you're not processing anymore, you're not thinking; you're witnessing. At that exact moment, you should simply be observing because in that instant all your processing has stopped. You're in the moment; you're in the zone.

"You've seen how your vision blurs when you move your head to look at something. On the court, you want to use your eyes, not your head, to track the ball. There are several things you can do to reduce head movement. First, don't stare at your opponent. If you're staring at her, half your potential visual field is above her and half below her. There is almost no utility in being able to see much above her because the ball ultimately is going to end up bouncing in front of you . . . unless your opponent has hit a lob. Instead look down toward the service line on your side of the court and then lift your eyes, not your head, to look across the net at your opponent. That allows you to see all you need to see of your opponent and her side of the court.

Dan, one of the instructors, is waiting at the baseline on the other side of the net. As I speak, we both demonstrate my words: "Your opponent gets ready to serve, and you're looking down at your service line. He tosses the ball up in the air, and you look up with your head. (There's a good chance your mouth has come open too.) Wrong. You watch the toss by

SPECIAL LESSON/SESSION

moving your eyes only. That ball is headed to your service box, and you won't be able to track it with your head jerking. If you're facing the service line, the ball is going to end up right in front of you without your moving your head.

"As soon as the ball leaves your opponent's racket, you're forming your *V* out in front of you. Lo and behold, when the ball reaches the impact point and you swing, you're looking straight at it. You don't have to jerk your head because you've been facing the impact point — not the net — during the entire flight of the ball. Also, you've tracked the ball with your eyes up and to the side, just where they should be to spark your mind to create your next shot.

"I watched Pete Sampras win his thirteenth Grand Slam title (and seventh Wimbledon), and whenever they showed a close-up of him waiting to return serve, you could see that he was looking across the net from the tops of his eyes. Has he been trained to do that? I don't know. Some people are naturals. It's possible that he developed his famous droopy-shoulder posture to bring his head down to where he needs to look out the tops of his eyes to see the serve; or it may be that his posture is an unconscious response. You see that head-down, humble posture among martial artists too. Of course, *humble* doesn't have to mean 'scared' or 'timid.' Remember Caine from 'Kung Fu'? Always humble, always confident.

"Tip number two. Don't lift your head to watch your own shot fly across the net. Keep your head down, and watch the shot with your eyes. If you

SPECIAL LESSON/SESSION

find yourself staring across the net with your head up, lower your head immediately and track the ball the rest of the way with your eyes. You may 'lose' the ball for an instant, but you'll recover and be more focused. Even on overheads, keep your head facing the projected impact point, which is slightly above you and forward, and watch the ball fall into view with eye movements, not head movements.

"Number three. Practice the shots you hit most often in combination. You want to have a store of Vs to choose from. Say in matches that you tend to serve and then volley. In practices, then, you should be working on your serve and volley together, not hitting serves and then hitting volleys. Look for other combinations in your game: approach shots and volleys, approaches and overheads, maybe a backhand baseline shot followed by a forehand winner up the line. Whatever shots you often hit in combination in your matches you should be practicing in combination. That should give you a ready store of Vs to choose from.

"Finally, remember the objective: Your job is never just to watch the ball. Your job is to envision a response to the ball flying toward you and then to make that vision happen. In the instant before you swing, you must have a good idea of what you want to happen in the next few seconds. The *V* is your prediction of the future, and creating the *V* is indeed the job of a seer."

I pause for a moment and then go on. "Now, I want to get back to a question that someone in this group asked: 'If you can't change your swing when the ball is close, why do you need to see the impact at all?' I gave you one reason in the last lesson: feedback. Seeing the impact gives you great nonconscious feedback for your body to learn from. Here's the other reason: You want to be in the moment. The more in the moment you are, the more likely you are to be in the zone. If you're not watching the impact, then by definition you're not in that moment and so cannot zone. If you're looking elsewhere, part of you is elsewhere. If you're seeing the impact, you're in the moment during the execution of the stroke and, by definition, zoned. Remember: Being zoned, which is the equivalent of being in the moment, is how we define *enlightenment*.

"Looking with the eyes, not the head, is a critical skill in other sports too. Most hitters in baseball keep their heads down; they follow the ball with their eyes, not their heads. They know the pitcher's target, so they know exactly what their field of vision needs to be. Of course, they're watching the pitcher's windup and delivery, but they're watching with their eyes. Their heads are facing the projected point of impact.

"In golf, looking with the eyes is less obvious. I believe a good golfer takes the club back and lets the momentum tip his chin slightly toward his back shoulder, so that he is staring down at the ball with the sides or tops of his eyes. As the swing comes down, he lets the momentum of the stroke drag his head forward, so that at impact his eyes are straight down facing the ball. Notice that throughout the shot, the ball is always the focus; but by tipping his chin naturally, the golfer has kept the ball in the proper

SPECIAL LESSON/SESSION

position in his eyes during the critical moments when the shot is being created. Then he allows his chin to come forward, naturally, with the downswing of the club. In this position, the ball returns to the center of his eyes at the moment of impact.

"So that's what I want you to practice today — hitting with your head down. You may find this takes some getting used to . . . particularly if humility isn't one of your strong suits. But don't worry. The instructors will be watching and calling out reminders."

Lesson 4

READER: **You too.**

We begin with a meditation. Some of the students have told me they're meditating on their own, which is great. The relaxation response will grow on them more quickly.

"Today I want to start you on a part of the New Age tennis process that involves some introspection, some self-analysis. I jokingly call this part *tennis therapy*.

"I had a student named Joe, and he always showed up late for his tennis lesson. And when he played, he always was late getting to the ball and getting his feet set. Hmm. Karen, another student, always forgot her wristband and checkbook. She was never prepared for her strokes on the court either. Hmm. Mike started and stopped taking lessons five times. Each time he'd say he was really going to stick to it this time. Strangely, all his strokes also lacked follow-through. All together now . . ."

The class joins me in a group Hmm.

"As a tennis teacher, I could devote my time to correcting on-court problems. I could have told Joe to set his feet, Karen to take a bigger backswing, and Mike to swing through the ball. Over the course of a one-hour lesson, I would have reminded them each twenty or more times. Over the course of several lessons, they might have heard the instruction hundreds of times.

"I see some of you smiling. I bet you've heard corrections like those a million times?"

One student raises her hand and says: "I don't bend my knees enough on my backhand, and I've heard about it since I was maybe seven years old."

Several others share similar memories.

"So why don't you fix it? Are you all just stubborn? Do you just keep forgetting? Maybe you don't understand the instruction? Maybe you don't really want to play better?"

I smile and shake my head no. "I don't think so. More likely, your strokes — your on-court behaviors — are just so natural to you, so much a part of you, that changing them is difficult.

"Of course the real problem isn't your strokes: It's whatever aspects of your personality that affect your strokes. The theory we use here is 'Let's see if we can change you so that you will begin to produce new natural strokes,' strokes that work better and still feel good.

"An example: Suppose you're a cautious person. Your natural strokes probably are cautious too. Maybe you allow the ball to get too close to you so that you feel more secure. Maybe you use a short, safe swing. Maybe you don't lean your body weight into the stroke. Maybe you don't go for your winners. The particular behavior doesn't really matter. It's just a product of your cautious personality. A tennis instructor should have no difficulty spotting your problem, or at least the manifestation of the problem in your strokes, and directing you not to get too close to the ball, to lean forward, and to swing through the ball. During the lesson, assuming you listen to the coach, you'll see definite improvement. Oh, every so often you'll forget; but the coach will remind you, and, by and large, you'll do much better. You'll leave the lesson feeling great, your new stroke in hand.

"But you're still a cautious person, and that caution must find an outlet somewhere on the court. Okay. The next time you're in a match, you're leaning forward and swinging through the ball, but suddenly you find yourself hitting safely up the middle. Or the first time you find yourself in a tense situation, say a third-set tiebreaker, your new swing is gone.

"The truth: The difficulties you're having on the court — the tight stroke, the poor body-weight transfer, the reluctance to hit winners — are just symptoms. And correcting the symptoms doesn't cure the underlying problem.

"You can pick up all kinds of tips from lessons and books: 'Let's see. I have to remember to toss the ball higher on my serves. On my forehand, I have to remember to hit out in front. On my backhand, I have to bend my knees. On volleys, I have to remember to keep my wrist firm. On my approach shots, . . .' If you've studied the game, you know how hard it is to remember each and every one of those tips in practice, never mind in matches and tournaments.

"Some coaches recommend that their students bring a written list of tips to matches and read it on changeovers. I think there's a better way. Don't get me wrong. Champions have been created through the physical-tips type of training. But that type of training is good for some players and not at all good for others. Some of us need to uncover the root of our on-court problems and then change that. If you want to hit a tennis ball less cautiously, you have to become a less-cautious individual. The key: If you can alter the trait even a little, your strokes are going to change spontaneously. Your swings will loosen up, you'll transfer your weight more easily, and you'll hit for winners because that's the way a less-cautious person plays. And best of all, your new stroke will be natural, a stroke that fits the new, less-cautious you. You won't have to keep a list in your head, no mental clutter. That's important to us because we're heading for a zone.

"So the concept behind tennis therapy is simple: If you alter the personality trait, you're going to alter the playing style. And there's a bonus: Once you alter that personality trait, other on-court problems related to that trait fix themselves. Suddenly you notice that you're tossing the ball on your serve higher and farther forward or that you're not waiting for overheads to bounce before you hit them or that your approach shots are getting deeper. Surprise! All of those behaviors reflect your personality too.

When you fixed your tendency to be overcautious, you fixed them as well. And good riddance.

READER: **You try this too.**

"Okay, we're going to do an exercise. I want you to imagine that you're the kind of person who always gets involved with a new activity before you've finished the last one. Maybe you often find yourself working on several projects at once. Or maybe you're just a little scatterbrained, so that in the middle of cooking supper, you remember you had to make a phone call, which you do, forgetting all about the food, which burns.

"Now, even if you're nothing like the person I've just described, I want you to think about how that personality type might show up on the tennis court."

I wait a minute or two and then say, "Time's up. Here's my list of tennis symptoms that I think could result from being scatterbrained." I hold up a large sheet of paper on which I've noted several symptoms:

● Before finishing one stroke, you move your feet to run for the next stroke.
● You take your eye off the ball too soon, to look up and see where your shot has gone.
● You don't finish off points, games, or sets well because you're always thinking about what's ahead.
● You cut short your follow-throughs.

- You lunge at your serve when you're trying to rush to the net.
- You run through your approach shots.

I read through the list. "You may have come up with others. If you find —."

"Hold it," calls out Beth, a young woman in the front. "I do every one of those things, some more often than others, but I do all of them. That's amazing. And I'm like that: I've always got fifty things working at once."

"Well, an Aha experience. We like those here. And you're all going to have one, a realization of some sort about how your personality is affecting your game. That's the point of this lesson, after all: getting you to think about your issues.

"You see, to increase your likelihood of zoning, you must be playing with the right attitude. I don't just mean that you want to win. Most players want to win. But we all have ways of hindering our own success; we all do things that stop us from achieving all we can achieve. Maybe we're too cautious or a little scattered or indecisive or even late. Those traits keep us from accomplishing all that we can.

"This part of the process is a means of getting you to learn about yourself. The method: in large part, psychological self-examination. That's right. We expect you to help uncover the traits that need fixing. I know you're not psychologists, but between Oprah and self-help books, you understand that sometimes you do things for reasons that aren't readily recognized by your conscious mind. And I'm pretty sure you all understand the tendency to repeat psychological patterns, to use defense mechanisms — like rationalizing and projection — to get past your 'little flaws.' At The Zone, we ask a question: What aspect of your personality keeps you from being all that you can be? Are you indecisive? Are you hesitant? Are you easily intimidated? Overly aggressive? Insecure? We're looking for your issue, your stuff. Is that stuff affecting your tennis game? You can bet on it.

"Okay. Remember in the first lesson I asked you to make a list of your tennis weaknesses? We're going to look at those lists now. I want you to see if you can think of a personality trait of yours that might account for most or all of the problems you listed. If you're stumped, try thinking about what you're like out in the 'real world.' If you're indecisive or shy or passive or whatever, that probably carries over to your tennis."

I stop and give the students a few minutes to look over their lists. In the meantime, members of the staff walk around to see if they can answer any personal questions. Some people don't like to share, at least not yet; so we just speak quietly with whomever asks.

After a bit, I ask for a volunteer: "Do any of you want to share your list to see if we can think of a possible trait together?"

Tim, a high school junior, raises his hand. "I wrote down that my serve is inconsistent because my toss is bad, that I hit crappy approach shots, that I always hit my backhands late, and that I double-fault late in matches or when I'm feeling pressure." He stops and then adds, "And sometimes my feet aren't set right. That's what I have." Another hesitation and then: "Oh, I left out crappy overheads."

I write the list on the board while Tim talks. Then I turn back to the students: "All right. Look at the weaknesses Tim listed. Can anyone think of a trait that might explain them?"

No hands.

"Tim, let me ask you a question. "When you hit your backhands late, are you thinking that you're just trying to get the shot back, that you're not going to do anything with it?"

"Yeah, I do that a lot."

"And when you double-fault late in a match, are you just trying to get your serve in the box?"

He nods. Several other students nod too.

"Are we seeing a pattern here? Let me try one more. On overheads, Tim, are you just trying to smash them, or are you trying to place them?"

"Most of the time just smash them," he says
"Does anyone see where I'm heading?"

A young woman raises her hand. "I know Tim; we go to school together. He was like the last one in our history class to choose a topic for this big report we had to do last term."

Tim chuckles. "That's funny. The day before we got here, I was rushing to finish a college application. It had to be postmarked that day."

"Okay, Tim, I'm getting a sense that you tend to put off making decisions. Am I right?"

"I guess that's me," he says. "So what do I do about it?"

"Good question. In a way, you've already taken the first step: understanding that your personality affects your play. Here are some practical exercises you can use. First, the next time you hit a bad shot, see if you can feel your indecisiveness. Did you have a target? Did you change your target at any point? Try to feel the difference between an indecisive stroke and a decisive one. Second, when you're serving your second serve, pick a definite spot in the box to aim at, and decide if you're going to hit the ball flat or with a spin. You want to make a decision — good or bad — on every shot because that's your issue. Third, I think you'll find that the Vs will help you focus and make you more decisive. Finally, get to know your indecisiveness. Notice it everywhere — when you're staring into the refrigerator trying to decide what to eat, when you're standing in the music store for fifteen minutes trying to choose between two CDs. There's more, but we'll get to that later."

Tim nods his head, and I thank him for sharing with us.

"Do mine," calls out Marla.

Before I can say anything, she begins reading her list: "I get stuck at the baseline in long rallies, I think because I stink at the net. Number two, I stink on approach shots. Number three, my first serve st—"

I interrupt: "Stinks?" I can't help myself.

She nods. "Yup, stinks. And for number four, I have that I don't finish off short balls."

"Okay, does anyone have a suggestion?"

"A different sport?" jokes one of Marla's friends.

"Come on, let's stick to positive feedback."

I wait a few seconds, but no hands go up.

"Let me tell you what I think it is." I turn to Marla: "I think that you have trouble on the strokes that require you to do something new. You're good at things that are routine, but you're not comfortable initiating your own ideas. Does that sound like you?"

"I think so."

"When you're not playing tennis, do you like to be the leader, the center of attention?"

"Not usually."

"Do you have any other hobbies, like music or art?"

"No. I have fish."

"And do you take care of them? Feed them? Keep the tank clean?"

"Yes, I do. And I guess I have a routine. I think you're right: I like routines. I don't really like it when things are out of whack."

"Well, routines are fine, but being creative will really add to your game. That's something you can work on here. Focus on being creative on those strokes that require you to be creative. The ones you mentioned —

approach shots and volleys and short balls — are a great place to start. Can you see that those strokes require you to be spontaneous, to think on your feet? When you're in a back-court duel, see if you can change the direction of the play. That will be a good challenge for you here."

Marla seems happy.

"The rest of you should study your lists and try to do what we've been doing. Remember, you're examining yourself: Use what you know about yourself, what you're like, to come up with a trait to work on. If you're indecisive off the court, chances are you're indecisive on the court. If you're overfond of routine off the court, chances are you're overfond of routine on the court. You've identified the symptoms; now find what's causing them.

"A word of caution though: You may have to do some digging. One of my students was a shy young man who would eagerly rush the net. Now, doesn't that contradict everything I've said? Why would a shy person rush the net? Rushing the net turned out to be a defense mechanism for him. He knew that the longer a point continued, the more pressure he would feel and the worse he would play. He rushed the net because he wanted to get it over with fast. Winning or losing the point was less important to him than relieving the pressure for a while. I found all this out when I asked him one day how he approaches giving a speech in front of a class. He said, 'I always volunteer to go first because I can't stand the wait. I just want to get it over with.' He would rush to the front of the class just like he would rush to the net. His anxiety produced both his shyness and his attack mode.

"We call that student's anxiety or Tim's indecisiveness or Marla's reliance on routine a *major life issue,* an MLI. What I want you to do is to get in touch with your MLI."

Again the instructors walk around and help each student find his or her issue. After a while, we're ready to head to the courts.

"Before we go play, I want to tell you about the best part of New Age tennis. What you learn here about yourself is going to change your behavior both on and off the court. Learning to be less cautious is going to strengthen your game; it's also going to make you more outgoing. Learning to follow through on the court may help you finish what you start off the court — a project, a course, a relationship. And that's the way it should be. Through this process, you will come to recognize and work on an aspect of your personality that needs changing, and that's a personal issue not a tennis problem. Anything you learn about yourself goes with you when you leave the court.

"Did I say that you can change your personality through New Age tennis? Well, you can. That's the whole idea. Even a small change in a single trait can mean large gains on and off the court. And once you get a taste of the benefits of self-discovery, you may find yourself hooked. You'll notice another trait, and you'll see the impact it has on your tennis and on your life. And pretty soon the point of playing tennis becomes much more than winning a game. The game becomes a life tool, a means of self-discovery on the path to life mastery."

With that we head out to the courts. On the way, the instructors and I talk about the MLIs the students have chosen. We agree with some of those choices; we think others may be off a little. The students' play will be the true test.

Session 4

I send the students onto the courts with one instruction: "Armed with your new understanding of yourself and your game, see if you can feel your challenge area while you play. I think you're going to like this."

First the players just rally. Because we want them to simply feel their game, we temporarily suspend practice seeing the *V*s. After about fifteen minutes, we ask them to play points against a partner, each player serving five in a row and then switching off. We watch to determine if the MLI each student picked during the lesson seems to fit. We stop and ask questions sometimes, but we try not to change anything about the students' natural swing . . . right now. Many of them are thrilled just to have an explanation for some of their problem strokes. And some are experiencing their issue. We hear comments like "Oh, was I ever indecisive on that shot!" and "Could I be more passive?"

We've encouraged the students to tell us about new insights or feelings on the court. One stops after a point and says to me, "When he comes to the net like that, I can feel my stomach tightening up." Another tells one of the other instructors: "I hit that shot, but until the last second I was going to hit a different shot." When that happens, we stop the play and speak to the players. We want to see if the insights or feelings fit the players' picture of themselves. We also want to get an overall sense of what they're thinking about on the court when they're not thinking about tennis. The students who reach out to us help the process along. Among those who don't are the players whose issues are subtle.

We spend the rest of the morning watching and speaking with the students about their MLIs. Several players make breakthroughs. One woman realizes that when she tosses the ball on her serve, she feels as though she's being critiqued — which is what her dad used to do when she'd practice — and that her anxiety has been making her settle for a safe, softer serve. This gets her thinking about how the feeling that she's being watched and judged constrains her life and how good she feels when she plays tennis with more abandon. An Aha like that is worth the price of admission.

Another student has come to see that he often lines up an aggressive stroke but, at the last second, backs off and goes for a safe shot, which he sometimes misses because he's not ready. And he has no problem finding an off-the-court corollary: He describes several trips he's planned and a business he'd hoped to start that he scuttled at the last moment.

Another man recognizes a problem we often see: His forehand is steady and consistent, but timid; his backhand is powerful but inconsistent. Like

Dr. Jekyll, he has two different personalities. The trigger is his level of comfort or confidence. When he's comfortable, he acts kind and somewhat timid. "Often" he tells one of the instructors, "I'm too kind when people need to be told something that might hurt them at work or at home." That's the same behavior he's exhibiting in his forehand, reliable and timid. But when he's in an uncomfortable situation, he can be "harsh and unpredictable," the behavior he's exhibiting in his backhand. He slices at the ball very firmly, almost angrily. And it's a wicked shot . . . when it hits the court. His forehand and backhand have become expressions of the two sides of his self, comfortable and anxious. He tells us that he likes the predictability of his forehand much more than his erratic backhand. Not surprisingly, he much prefers his forehand behavior on and off the court. We talk to him about finding a middle ground.

Some students are not comfortable with the MLI they've identified, but that is to be expected. To help them along, the instructors compare the students' scores on the targeting exercise in Session 1 with the traits each player has picked. At The Zone, we've found that MLIs have a strong impact on targeting.

Here is some of what we look for:*

* These are not one-to-one correlations. Approach shots, for example, also can reflect a player's shyness.

- When a player's targeting scores are low on approach shots, the underlying problem often is indecisiveness; approach shots call for decisiveness.
- High volleying scores usually are associated with spontaneity or creativity.
- People who think too much tend to have trouble targeting overheads.
- Low scores on serves usually indicate the underlying trait of procrastination.

Our logic: If players routinely have trouble creating a good, clear target on a certain type of stroke — backhands, for example — then their minds are busy thinking about something else at the moment they should be thinking about the target. We've also found that the strokes the players have difficulty targeting tend to be their problem strokes, their "bad" strokes. It's not that the underlying trait — whatever it is that has them thinking about something else when they should be thinking about targeting — goes away when they hit one of their "good" strokes. More likely, their comfort with a good stroke allows them to set the negative thought or feeling pattern aside and to concentrate on their target. That ability to focus disappears on bad strokes, when the negative thoughts or feelings are reinforced with performance anxiety, leaving the players with no room to think about their target.

If just one stoke doesn't seem to fit a student's MLI, other issues may be at play. (I talk about this more in Lesson 6.) But if we find several strokes unaccounted for by an MLI, we reexamine the students' MLI choice.

We encourage the students to pay particular attention to what they're thinking about when they hit one of their problem strokes, the strokes on which they scored lowest in the targeting exercise. We do everything we can to get them to feel the connection between their MLI and their strokes:

- "Feel your hesitation. Did you move for the ball instantly? Did you hit the ball as far forward as you would like? Does your stroke have a pause in it?"
- "Your indecisiveness is showing. Notice how often you fail to make a clear decision about where and how to hit the ball."
- "See if you can feel the anxiety that comes from approaching the net or hitting a hard overhead. Notice how safe you feel behind the baseline."

At first we don't have the students change anything. We simply want them to recognize and feel the effect of their issue on their play. Later in the session, as an exercise, we ask them to play differently, out of character: "We want you to change your game by putting on a new personality. Try to play like someone else whose game you know — a friend or even a tennis personality." After a few minutes, we tell the students to go back to their own game.

During a break, I ask: "Did you feel a change in personality when you were playing out of character? What did it feel like to go back to your own game? What were the differences?"

I can see several students struggling with their answers. "That's okay," I say. "You don't have to put your answers into words. This is 'feel language.' You must begin by feeling what it is to play tennis as you, with your unique mindset."

I send them back to the courts: "Play a little longer, and see if you can find other difficulties, ones you haven't written down, that can be explained by the major life issue you've chosen. Sometimes you have to examine your behavior before a match, not just during it. Do you bring everything you need to a match? Do you warm up enough? Stretch? If not, why? Could it be your MLI showing up? Are you prepared — on and off the court? Or are you late setting your feet and getting your racket back? Is that a behavior you see in your work or at home? Do you meet deadlines? Do you get bulbs in the ground before the first frost? If the issue you've chosen is indeed your MLI, you should have no trouble finding examples." To help students uncover problem behaviors in competition, we set up a match. Again we're looking for common problems:

● Failing to finish off points. Many players can hit everything but the "finisher."
● Pulling back at the end of a game. Some players lose games they

should win easily because they begin to play too conservatively when they're ahead.

- Missing put-aways. When players are looking ahead, they can't focus on the present.
- Being intimidated by an opponent or stroke. For example, many players freeze up on passing shots when their opponent rushes the net.

We individualize the matches as much as possible, bearing in mind the students' specific issues. We might take a player who feels intimidated when his opponent rushes the net and pair him with a player who's trying not to be her usual passive self, urging the passive player to go to the net at every opportunity. The goal of this exercise, of the whole session: to help the students connect to the emotions they're experiencing when they play tennis.

We take special notice of the five we identified in our first conference. First Marla. She does very well under the usual, physical type of tennis instruction; she just seems to have hit a plateau. She is very predictable: She's good on routine shots and weak on shots that require initiative — net shots, approaches, and short balls. (Actually, she does better with her weak strokes in doubles, where the structure of the play is more predictable.) Marla is having a problem with the MLI concept. First, she doesn't feel comfortable with the self-examination that's an integral part of tennis therapy. More important, we're asking her to change, and a reluctance to change is part of her issue. Right now, we're letting her blame her difficulty with the process on what she calls her "spaciness." But I don't think she's spacey. I think she acts that way so that others don't expect much from her, so that she doesn't have to think for herself. I am going to meet with her later and work on her defense mechanisms. We try to take players only as far as they can comfortably go . . . but at least that far.

Diane is at the other end of the spectrum. She's an artist, and her creativity shows up in her work, in the clothes she wears, in the color of her hair, and, yes, in the decisions she makes on the tennis court. To make the game more interesting, she often chooses a difficult shot over a perfectly good routine shot, and that costs her points on the court.

To help Diane see the impact her decision making — with a bit of rebelliousness thrown in — is having on her game, the day after the first session we asked her to play a set while we videotaped her. Afterward, we picked out seven shots she hit that clearly were bad choices, each more difficult and less effective than another option. Another factor in our choosing the seven shots: Diane lost five of the points and could easily have lost the other two.

How significant are 5 or 7 points in a set? Well, most competitive sets are between 50 and 70 points. Statistically, because of the way tennis is scored — points leading to games, leading to sets, leading to a match —

players don't get credit for every point they score. If they're winning 25 percent of the points, they probably won't win any games; in fact, they'll lose most games 4–0, 4–1, or 4–2. Big servers aside, players probably need to win at least 35 percent of the points to win a game. In a 6–4 set, the losing player probably won 45 percent or more of the points. That means that in a 60-point set, the losing player could easily have won 27 points to the winner's 33 points. A swing of 5 points would put the loser ahead 32 to 28. Even in a 6–2 set, the losing player could have won 40 percent or more of the points, 24 points to 36. A swing of 6 points, and the set would have been dead even.

As we watched Diane on tape, she attempted a heavy-topspin sharp-angled "roller" that went wide, when all she had to do was push the ball over the net. She tried a very difficult passing shot, with almost no hope, when a lob was definitely in order. And she double-faulted several times trying to put so much spin on her second serve that it didn't clear the net — this despite the fact that her opponent hadn't been doing any damage against her second serves.

When we showed the tape to Diane, we were careful to applaud her creativity, but we also made clear that sometimes the easy stroke produces the best results. One of the instructors explained that by choosing more-difficult strokes over routine strokes, Diane is limiting her options every bit as much as players who always opt for comfort. And when another instructor suggested that in a way Diane is letting others dictate what she does on the court, his words really hit home. Of course Diane likes the idea that her personality influences her tennis, and so is working on her issue willingly. We're all optimistic.

David is well aware of his overactive mind and is very willing to change. The problem: He's never been able to slow his thoughts down. After every mistake — on and off the court — he relives the mistake and then can't help thinking why he made it and how to prevent it from happening again. Although David worries, he's not our usual worrier: He's not fearful or easily intimidated. Instead he worries through overplanning. Hesitancy is also a form of worrying but is more mindless. Players with overactive minds seem to do well with New Age tennis. His willingness to change is also a key factor in the success of the technique.

Marty needed our help to find his MLI. He actually seemed relieved when we told him he's a dreamer: "That's a negative I can live with," he said. We explained that he has high, even unrealistic expectations of his "big" strokes (forehand, serve, and overhead) and low expectations of his weak strokes (the "grunt" strokes — backhands, second serves, and service returns). On the court, he looks as though he's waiting for just the right shot on which to unload. Marty's expectations of life manifest in other areas too. When he applied to college, for example, he was hoping for a tennis scholarship — a not very realistic goal — and he had no backup plan in place for paying for his education if a scholarship didn't come through. Our task is to help him see how unrealistically low his expectations — he believes that he "could never hit a winner off that stuff, anyway" — are for most of his strokes and how different he feels when he's unloading a big stroke. We want him to do more with his weak strokes just to feel what that's like and to see if all of his big shots are both wise and necessary. David isn't much of a feeler, but he has some understanding of psychology and is willing to try.

Henry knows he needs to open up. He seems angry but avoids speaking about his anger, so we're working very gently around the issue. He knows that he's stressed on the court, but he feels stress is a natural condition for high achievers and that he handles it pretty well. When pressed about opening up, he admits that he never does "silly things" and that he "takes the game too seriously." We had images of flying rackets, which he confirms with a smirk. We're going to start him working on loosening up his swing. We want him to recognize the ease of swinging with an I-don't-care attitude. I expect his play will suffer a bit at first and that we're going to have to encourage him not to care.

Lesson 5

The class begins with a meditation, but with a twist.

"Those of you who have meditated before probably have had someone guide you by asking you to imagine yourself in a beautiful garden or in a park next to a lake. How many of you know what I mean?"

Twelve students raise their hands.

"Most of you. That's good. For the rest of you: When you're learning to meditate, your teacher may ask you to close your eyes and picture yourself someplace beautiful. That's supposed to jump-start you on your way to relaxation. Today, I'm going to do a slight variation on the method."

I pause and then, in my deepest voice, say, "Please close your eyes."

I pause again and then go on: "You are alone on a tennis court."

That always gets a few giggles.

"It's sunrise, and there isn't a soul around. There's a bench on the side of the court. You decide to sit down and take a rest. You love being on the court. The court has been a source of much pleasure for you. You find balance here — physical, psychological, and spiritual balance.

"It is so peaceful sitting on the bench that you decide to close your eyes and meditate. You begin your alternate-nostril breathing and instantly grow calm, more at peace than you've ever been before. Meditate now. I'll let you know when the time is up."

After about eighteen minutes, I say, "Okay, take a moment and then open your eyes. Is everyone back?"

Some students nod or say yes immediately; others are slower to answer.

"Today we're going to talk about what happens to you physically and emotionally when you see a tennis ball coming at you. My contention is that you respond emotionally to the sight of the ball in flight before you consciously see it.

"Let me explain. Suppose someone throws a rock at your head. What do you do? You duck. That reaction is a kind of reflex, not altogether different from your leg's jumping when your doctor taps your knee. About now, some of you are saying to yourselves, 'But the knee-jerk reaction is automatic: You don't control it. When someone throws a rock at you, you see the rock and then you duck.' Right? Well, yes and no. Actually, your nonconscious mind sees the rock before you do and starts working on a response before you know what's happening.

"Wait a minute. Did I say that your nonconscious mind sees the rock before you do? Yes. That's the way human beings are designed."

I hold up a picture (Figure 10). "Okay. A short lesson in anatomy and

Figure 10
The visual cortex

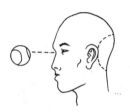

The visual cortex is at
the rear of the brain.

physiology. When light energy enters your eye, it passes through a lens and then is projected onto receptor cells that pass the impulse — the information contained in the light energy — on to the optic nerve. The optic nerve ultimately ends in the visual cortex, the part of the brain where you consciously see an image. Before the impulse gets to the visual cortex, though, it passes through alertness centers, motion centers, memory centers, and emotion centers. The last thing — literally — you were designed to do is to actually see the image. If you were meant to see the image first, the visual cortex would be located right behind your eyes, and it isn't. Actually, that's a good thing. If someone's throwing a rock at you and you have to think before you duck, you're going to end up with a big bump on your head. There's plenty of time after the rock misses for you to think, 'Boy, that was a rock.' You need to respond first and think second. And that's exactly how you're built.

"If you're afraid of snakes, the sight of a snake arrives at your consciousness with that fear attached. And if you're afraid of backhands, the sight of a backhand arrives at your consciousness with *that* fear attached. Your emotional response to an image sets in before conscious thought has any chance to get involved. That's why telling yourself 'Watch the ball' or 'Don't be nervous' is useless.

"The ball leaves your opponent's racket. You haven't actually seen it yet, but already you're responding to it. What kind of response are you having? If your opponent has hit an easy shot, something you feel confi-

107 LESSON 5

dent about returning, you probably are feeling good. If the shot is a challenging one, you probably are feeling less positive. Here we call those negative thoughts *Uh-oh backhands* or *Oh-no overheads*. Can anyone relate?"

Let the record show that everyone related.

"Some emotional and intellectual reactions help you produce good shots; others definitely get in the way of your game. And some of those disruptive reaction patterns are a function of your major life issue. Suppose your MLI is shyness, and it affects your game when you're forced to hit passing shots. You might not hear your thoughts during those shots, but they probably sound something like this: 'He's coming to the net again. Now I have to hit a passing shot. Uh-oh, he's covering the net pretty well. Gosh, I guess I'll just lob again.' This kind of response is a symptom of your shyness.

"Suppose you're indecisive. Your opponent fires off a shot and you're thinking 'I'm going to go for a winner up the line. No, the angle's not good; I'll hit a dink. Oh, now I don't know what to do.' And then you miss your shot.

"The point is your MLI is running around in your head dictating your responses. In time, those responses become behavior patterns or habits . . . bad habits. Before you're even conscious of the stimulus, you're automatically responding to it with counterproductive behavior. An example: If you're afraid to hit backhands, you're never going to try a difficult passing shot because it won't be an option in your mind. The fear limits your choices on and off the court.

"By now you have some insight into your MLI and the responses that are adversely affecting your tennis. So, here's the solution: Just stop being afraid or angry."

Several students laugh out loud.

"As some of you clearly are aware, it's not that easy. You can't just order your nonconscious mind around. You know how silly it sounds when someone tells you, 'Don't be nervous'? Well it's equally silly to tell your nonconscious to be more aggressive or decisive. Shyness and indecisiveness aren't simply add-ons to your personality; they're integral to it. You must attack the problem at a very basic level: You have to communicate directly with your nonconscious.

"You've already taken the first step by recognizing that a personality trait is at the root of your on-court problems. That recognition tells your nonconscious mind that change is coming. Your nonconscious mind — which has known all along that your conscious thoughts were interfering with your performance — is going to be very pleased when it discovers it has an ally on the outside, namely you. Your conscious mind has been feeding you distortions for so long, and you've been believing most of them. 'I just can't hit that shot,' 'I'm just not good at the net,' 'I'm always screwing up my serve' — what does any of that mean? Do you really believe that you don't have the physical potential to hit a good serve? If that's the case, you need to find another sport. As soon as you begin to act as though you understand that a particular personality trait is keeping you from serving well, you've come a long way toward serving better. Every time you serve, you must convey to your nonconscious mind that you have a new way of feeling and that you like it better than the old way. Do you procrastinate? What do you think procrastination looks like on a tennis court? One thing it can look like is a bad serve. Once you approach serving with the conviction that you want to get over procrastinating, you're motivated to change. But just saying 'Don't procrastinate' is like saying 'Don't be nervous.' You've got to speak to your nonconscious in what we call *feel language.'*

"The technique I use is a kind of self-programming: It involves pairing an emotional response with a new thought, to achieve a new emotional response. The point of the technique is to be sure that your nonconscious mind has a new thought or feeling pattern available to it whenever it decides to kick the old one.

"I need two volunteers."

I choose a man and a woman intentionally.

"Thank you. Here's what I'd like you to do. I'm going to ask you to walk a certain way. Whatever it is, please do it immediately. Don't think about it; just do it. Okay, walk like a tough guy, a bully."

The two begin to swagger around the room.

After a minute, I say, "Okay, now walk like a sexy woman, a flirt."

Immediately they tilt their heads and begin swinging their hips as they walk. Some of the students laugh.

"Let me ask you a question. When I told you to walk like a bully, did you stop to think about each individual change you would make in your walk — lifting your shoulders, pushing your chest out, lengthening your stride — or did you just think 'tough guy' and then walk?"

They both agree that they didn't think about the details. The woman says, "I just sort of put on a feeling of tough inside, and it came out outside."

"And if I asked you to do it again, could you?"

Both students say yes.

"Of course you could. Walking tough or sexy is a simple example of how you can alter a physical act, a habitual physical act, simply by putting on a new attitude. So why can't you alter your tennis stroke by hitting with a new attitude? Well, you can. Suppose we were on the court, and I asked any one of you to hit the ball as though you were crazy. Can you feel yourselves whacking at the ball? Or suppose I asked you to play as though you were very scared? Can you feel the tight little strokes you'd use? My point: By changing your attitude, you can change the way you hit.

"You probably can see where I'm going with this. Suppose I ask you to play with an attitude that would improve your game: 'Play more assertively,' 'Play more decisively,' 'Play more efficiently.' Could you change the way you play just by changing your attitude?"

Several students are nodding.

"Of course you can, but the process isn't quite as easy as hitting wildly or timidly. The reason: You don't have a precise image of what your swing would look like if you were just a bit more assertive or a bit more decisive.

"So what we're going to do is find an image for you to use. To start, I want you to think about your MLI and its impact on one aspect of your game. Then I want you to think of a situation off the court that mirrors the problem you're having on the court. For example, suppose that timidity is your MLI and that it's affecting your serve. Your off-the-court example might be 'When I'm with friends and they ask me where I want to eat, I usually just say that I don't care. But I usually do think of someplace I'd like to eat; I'm just shy about saying so.'

"If you're having trouble coming up with a real-life example, my first thought is that you may not have found your major life issue. Your MLI should show up in many of your behaviors. But if you think you've got the trait right and just can't come up with an example, make one up.

"It's important to make the image clear, to see yourself with your friend discussing lunch, for example. Now, once you've got a scene that conveys your MLI, rerun the scene in your mind. Imagine the same situation — the same scene — but this time with you reacting differently. When your friend asks where you want to eat, maybe you say, 'You know, I don't usually care where we eat, but today I'm really in the mood for Italian food.' Think through the reenactment so that it feels right to you. That's important. You must be comfortable with the new response. If you're not ready to say that you're in the mood for Italian food, picture yourself saying, 'Well, I was thinking maybe Italian or Chinese. What do you think?' At a later date, you can change the story to make yourself even less timid. You want to be as comfortable as you can but still challenge yourself. It's a fine line.

"One more thing. The revised story should trigger a physical or emotional response in you. Maybe you smile, stand up straighter, or hold your head differently, or maybe you just feel a sense of accomplishment or pride. That's very important. It's that change — that physical or emotional response — that is going to help you change your behavior on the court.

"What you're looking for here is a memory that you can draw on to disrupt your MLI. I've been describing how to create that memory; but if you already have one, use it. Maybe at lunch today you caught yourself being indecisive or being too aggressive, and you said to yourself, 'No, I'm not going to be like that.' And you spoke up or let someone else have a turn talking, and you felt good about it. Well, use that memory. That's the best kind of memory to draw on.

"Once you create or remember a scene in which you've faced down your MLI, I want you to take the physical or emotional sensation of your victory with you to the court. The best way to do that is to come up with a short phrase — 'Italian food' — or an image — a plate of pasta — that helps you relive the scene and all of your feelings.* When you want to induce the feel-

---

* Actually, you can use a tune or a scene from a movie, anything that evokes a good feeling.

ing of being more decisive or of being less aggressive, you only have to think that phrase or see that image.

"Remember that the phrase or image has to convey a feeling, not a meaning. 'Italian food' has to evoke something very real in you, and I don't mean hunger. The phrase or image must help you experience the scene again *and* must produce the sensation — physical or emotional — your success evoked. Psychologists call this kind of phrase or image a *mediating thought*. A mediating thought helps you recreate a specific feeling.

"It is impossible to separate physical sensations and emotional responses. Smile. Do it, smile. Do you feel a wave of happiness? They are connected. Act proud. Go ahead, do it. Did you straighten up? When you're proud, you straighten up. And when you straighten up, I bet you feel proud. The sensation and response are related. In you, there's an emotional feeling (feeling less timid) and a physical feeling (a feeling that's unique to each individual) that go together. You're looking for a story that produces pairs of feelings.

"Most of you, I'm sure, know about Pavlov and his dog. Pavlov was a researcher studying a type of learning called *conditioning*. He knew that certain stimuli trigger an automatic response — a dog sees food and salivates, for example. Was it possible, he wondered, to produce the response through training? Could he train a dog to salivate to the sound of a bell? The answer, of course, was yes. Pavlov would ring a bell and then bring food out to the dog, and the dog would salivate. The researcher always rang the bell before setting the food in front of the dog. Eventually, the dog salivated to the sound of the bell alone.

"What does Pavlov's story have to do with tennis? The answer has to do with learning. He showed us that any stimulus, even a bell ringing, could be paired with an instinctive reaction, like salivating, and that in time the stimulus would trigger the reaction. In effect, what Pavlov did with the bell, you can do with the sight of a tennis ball."

I write a diagram on the chalkboard (Figure 11).

"The idea is to train yourself through repetition. As your opponent begins to swing his or her racket, you think your mediating thought. That

Figure 11
Learning new responses

Pavlov

Dog learns:	Bell > Food > Salivation (*repeat*)
Then dog learns:	Bell > Salivation

Tennis

Player learns:	Opponent swings at ball > Mediating thought > New reaction (*repeat*)
Then player learns:	Opponent swings at ball > New reaction

phrase or image disrupts your old response pattern, the pattern that includes all your timidity and other stuff. And once you disrupt the pattern, the new sensation is right there to replace the old one. The upshot: You're playing better tennis.

"It's important that you don't just think your mediating thought; you have to feel it too. Feel the pride, the satisfaction, of communicating your will directly. 'Italian food.' Now express that feeling with your racket.

"You need the feeling to change both your attitude and your game. How can you be sure you've got the feeling? One clue is the physical sensation that you associate with your mediating thought. If you're feeling it, you should be smiling or standing up straighter or doing whatever it is you do when you're being more decisive.

"Look at the diagram again. Notice that repetition is a critical component of the initial training. When you set out to disrupt your MLI, you must think the mediating thought on every stroke you hit. Every stroke, not just your problem strokes. That's the only way you're going to break your bad habit.

"Right now, there's a very close bond between the sight of the ball coming off your opponent's racket and your feelings of shyness, indecisiveness, or whatever. They happen almost simultaneously. To break that bond, you have to get something in between them. The mediating thought is that something, and it's a powerful tool. It not only disrupts your counterproductive response; it gives you a new sensation to replace it. The result?

A new, less timid stroke that feels natural. And each time you hit the ball with that stroke and it works, your new attitude and behavior are being reinforced. That means you'll find it easier to evoke the new sensation the next time. It's a very positive cycle.*

"Again, it's important that any phrase you use as your mediating thought be suggestive, not instructional. 'Don't hesitate,' for example, doesn't work because it produces thoughts, not feelings. 'Italian food' is good because it has no meaning on the tennis court other than the feeling you associate with it.

"And what if you've wracked your brain and still can't come up with a mediating thought that evokes the feeling you're looking for? Well, start with any thought or image or tune that makes you feel good about yourself. Right now you want something, anything, that's going to disrupt your old pattern of responding. Over time, as your attitude changes, you'll have lots of positive experiences to choose from in deciding on a new mediating thought. And again, actual experiences make the best mediating thoughts.

"Finally, don't beat up on yourself when you forget to think your mediating thought or don't really feel it. You're just learning. At first, if you feel the sensation once every few strokes, you're doing well. It may take some time before you feel it in most situations. Remember that you're displacing

---

* Players can get some benefit from just thinking the mediating thought; more, from feeling it.

a pattern that has been popping into your head spontaneously for as long as you've been playing tennis. It's going to take time and some effort to move that pattern out."

We spend the rest of the lesson helping the students develop a mediating thought. Then we head out to the courts.

Session 5

The session begins with the students practicing hitting and using their mediating thoughts. Before they head onto the courts, I talk to them about timing: "Don't think your mediating thought too early, or your mind will find the time to push in your old response pattern. Just before your opponent swings is best for most players."

I continue: "And, to start, I don't want you to worry about seeing your Vs. I just want you to concentrate on your mediating thoughts." Later in the session, when the students are comfortable with their mediating thought, we ask them to reintroduce the Vs.

"Here's what we'd like you to do. You've just hit the ball, and it's flying toward your opponent. You're watching it with your eyes, not your head. Just before your opponent swings, I want you to think your mediating thought. Timing is crucial: You want to be feeling your new attitude just before your opponent swings; then, your focus should shift immediately to the V.

"You know the targeting drill: As soon as your opponent hits the ball, start creating your *V*. See the trajectory of your return shot. Then, as the ball comes closer, add its trajectory toward you and the point of impact. Again, you're watching the ball with the tops and sides of your eyes; your head is facing the point of impact.

"As the ball gets closer, finalize your *V*. Watch the line in the air that represents the shot you want to hit, and see it intersect with the line in the air that represents the ball's flight toward you. That's your *V*.

"Now, with the ball just feet in front of you and you locked into your *V*, move your eyes ever so slightly forward from the ball to the *V*. The ball should enter your visual focal point a second later, when your eyes are fixed and steady and you can clearly see the impact. When you're ready, swing.

"As soon as the ball is headed back toward your opponent, get ready to think your mediating thought again.

"One more thing. When it works — when you've timed your mediating thought just right, formed your *V*, and feel good about the shot you've made — take a mental bow. It's important to reward yourself for facing down your MLI and seeing the *V* . . . even if the ball sails over the fence. Feel good because you were right there in the shot, all of your mental skills working.

"Some of you probably are thinking, 'Wait a minute. If I'm using my mediating thought and seeing the *V*, why would I hit the ball badly?' The answer: You're in training. Feeling differently and seeing the *V* are just the first steps in the process. Your body needs a little time to figure out how the new you hits the ball. The best way to speed up the process is by not expecting too much at first. Right now you simply want to enjoy the sensation of doing it right. Maybe you're less anxious; maybe you're more excited about hitting the ball or more inclined to go for winners; or maybe you're just having more fun. Don't worry about your overall performance just yet. Instead concentrate on the good feeling you get when you hit the ball with the right attitude and focus. Your physiology will catch up, I promise you.

"What you don't want to do is create confusion. What do I mean? You know that many times you can hit a good shot by accident, without focus or planning. Even though you don't hit the shot you intended, it's a winner. Now, if you reward yourself each time that happens, in short order you'll be trying to reproduce whatever it is you've been doing. That's only natural.

"But there are two problems with that. First, reproducing a fluke is a thankless task. You were lucky, that's all. Second, and more important, you don't want to reinforce the lack of concentration that led up to an accidental winner.

"Of course everyone likes a gift. But you don't want to reward yourself for any shot you make by accident. From now on, pat yourself on the back only when you've thought your mediating thought and seen a *V*. That's the only way to get your body to do what it has to do. Don't rate your shots based on how they come out. If your attitude was good and you were seeing a good *V*, you should reward yourself no matter where the ball lands.

"Some of you are going to notice an immediate change for the better in your game. For others, it's going to take a little time before you see a correlation between your new attitude and your shots. But don't give up: Keep rewarding yourself for your mental effort, and you'll see your performance changing."

With that, the students head back to the courts to practice both mediating thoughts and *V*s.

●

After the session, the instructors meet to talk over the students' progress. Much of the discussion focuses on the five students we've been tracking.

Diane's mediating thought is "Just do the job." I didn't like it at first because it sounds a lot like "Be decisive" or "Don't be nervous" — phrases that are more likely to get a player thinking than feeling. But Diane has a specific job in mind, a part-time job she had one summer. Although the work was routine, she felt good at the end of the day. One clue that this is the right mediating thought for her: the smile on her face when she told me the story. I like to look for visible changes, particularly in students' expressions, posture, or stance.

Marla is becoming a "special" special case. We realized early on that spaciness isn't her MLI; that her real issue is her lack of will, her inability to take the initiative. Dan's description of working with Marla to help her understand her issue and to create a mediating thought sounds a lot like Abbott and Costello's "Who's on First" routine: "So I said to her that I thought she has trouble making changes.* And she said yes, but she doesn't really want to change by way of a mediating thought. So I pointed out to her that the reason she doesn't want to use a mediating thought is probably that she doesn't like change. To which she answered, 'Well, I'm uncomfortable doing that.'"

Before the lesson ended, I spent some time talking to Marla. She seemed open to the idea that her lack of will is hurting her tennis: She admits that she likes the security of the backcourt, that moving forward makes her nervous because "you never know what's going to happen." Given a choice, she says, she would always choose to start the point and just see who can maintain a baseline rally the longest. And she has no difficulty coming up with off-the-court examples. Although she's popular, she doesn't want to lead; she simply doesn't want to make any group's decisions. She told me that all her boyfriends have picked her, that she didn't pick any of them. Her lack of will

* Resistance to change is a common symptom of a lack of will.

in social situations seems to have its roots in her family situation: Her parents and older brothers are all very insistent that things be done a certain way, their way. They've never encouraged her to spread her wings.

In working with me to come up with a mediating thought, Marla had real trouble remembering or rescripting any situation with her being more forceful. Finally she remembered an argument with her father several years back. She wanted to wear a new turtleneck shirt to a match, but her father insisted she'd be too warm. Usually she would give in, but this time she stuck to her guns and went off in the new shirt. She laughed as she told me the story. "It was really hard for me," she said, "but I felt so brave wearing that shirt." We'd found Marla's mediating thought.

Unhappily, that was only half the battle. Marla announced that her mediating thought, the whole process, made her feel "incredibly silly." By the time we got to the courts, she had agreed to try to think and feel "turtleneck" just before her opponent hit the ball. But in short order, she stopped. Her excuse: She was hitting poorly. And despite our assuring her that her performance isn't what counts at this stage, she was adamant.

Marty's mediating thought is "I can do that." He remembered an algebra class he had mastered with the help of a tutor. We hoped the pleasure of bringing new skills to bear on a subject would encourage him to utilize all of his strokes, not just to dream and wait for a big forehand — a shot, by the way, that misses almost as often as it wins.

In the lesson it was clear that Henry isn't quite ready for a mediating thought. He insisted it would break his concentration. Looking for something to relieve his tension when he plays, we suggested that he exhale on every one of his strokes. He had no problem doing that during the practice. In fact, he would laugh now and again when his breathing out sounded more like a grunt than a breath. We picked up on it and encouraged him to use the grunt like a mediating thought, to make the noise just as his opponent hit the ball. He smiled every time he grunted, so I knew he was feeling something. It's a start.

David came up with the mediating thought "Get it done." When one of the instructors pointed out that the phrase doesn't evoke a feeling, David shared the story behind the phrase, a basketball coach who would use the expression "Go out there, and get it done." "Besides," he said, "I like that it makes me feel like I have to do something, not just think." In the session his hitting was erratic, but he was comfortable with the new feeling and is confident he can find his game. "The good ones feel real good," he told us. That's a comment we often hear at this stage in the process.

●

The next morning, the players start the day with matches that we've arranged. That gives them a chance to put their new techniques into action.

Lunch Break

Over lunch, the instructors and I sit around discussing how far each of the students has progressed and where they go from here. Marla is a big concern. She seems unwilling to alter her play. That might change, though: She lost badly to Diane in the match they played this morning, and the two had been very comparable earlier. After the match she admitted that she had not used the techniques. She said she isn't comfortable with them yet, but she promised to try when she's drilling. We'll see how she does in this afternoon's session.

Diane is smitten by the *V*. It gives her creative mind something to do. The *V* also helps Marty stop dreaming and do something with each of his strokes. Mentally he seems more present.

David has remembered an occasion when he was spontaneous, and he wants to change his mediating thought. The story involves skinny-dipping; and when he says "Bathing suit," there's a big grin on his face — always a good sign.

At a nearby table, I can hear several students talking with excitement about their play. Initially Marla joins in. Then, in a complete reversal, she admits that so far her game is way off, that she isn't "getting it." I can see how hard it is for her to say that. It might be a breakthrough for her. Speaking out that way is the most independent thing I've seen her do since she arrived. The others assure her she's going to catch on.

As lunch ends, I look up and see David making his way over. I think he's wanted to talk to me all during the meal; he knows he has to do it now because I'm getting up to leave. His behavior is textbook. On the court, he often hits a ball just before its second bounce. It's that wait-for-the-last-minute tendency that fits the "overthinker" so perfectly. And if you over-think one place, you do it lots of places.

"Excuse me, Robert, can I talk to you for a minute?"

"Only if you'll answer this question honestly."

"Okay."

"Tell me what your thought process was like while you were deciding to come speak to me."

He grins and then hems and haws.

"Well, I was going to come sooner, but at one point John came over and spoke to you, so I —"

I cut in, "For about thirty seconds."

"Okay, then I thought, well, you probably want your privacy at lunch. Then I thought that maybe we'd get to what I wanted to ask you today any-way, and it would be silly to ask. Then I thought —"

I cut in again, "David, what you were thinking really isn't important. What's important is that you went through the process. Finally, just as lunch is breaking up, you came over. Isn't that just like when you hesitate and then barely get to a ball? It's the same tendency to think and think until the last possible moment, and then rush to do whatever it is — talk to me or hit the ball."

"I guess I do it everywhere," he moans.

"Don't beat up on yourself. You now see your overthinking in a new light. What a great opportunity to deal with it."

That thought seems to please him, and he turns to go.

"David," I call after him, "what did you want to talk to me about?"

He laughs and says, "I think I already got my answer."

Lesson 6

READER: **You too.**

"Good morning. Please get comfortable, and let's settle into a meditation."

About eighteen minutes later, I say: "Welcome back. Before we go on, a couple of things. First, if any of you had any insights last night that you would like to share with an instructor, just let us know and we'll make sure you get a chance to talk with someone. Second, nothing is forever, not even your mediating thought. Over time, you may want to challenge yourself more. And at some point, you're going to feel that you've done all you want to do with your MLI, that it's time to move on to another aspect of your personality. So you create or remember a new mediating thought. I wouldn't change them daily, at least not after you've fixed on a good one; but you should start to feel when your phrase or image needs replacing. Any questions?"

A hand goes up. I point to Elizabeth, and she takes the floor.

"I just want to say something about my MLI. Last night I went down to late snack, and I picked through the herbal teas for twenty minutes trying to choose one. And this morning I caught myself trying to decide what to wear. It was pitiful. I only have a few things with me, and still I stood there for fifteen minutes choosing one thing and then another. But I *noticed,* and that's what's important. I know I'm indecisive, but I've never been so aware of it or so resolved to stop. That's it. I'm done."

Several of the students clap. Elizabeth sits down, grinning from ear to ear

"Does anyone else want to share something about an MLI or mediating thought?"

Marty raises his hand — I'm a little surprised — and then stands and says: "More than a few times in my life I've been accused of not trying my hardest, of not really paying attention to whatever it is that I'm doing. I, of course, always thought I had been doing my best. Well, I've discovered here that I'm a dreamer, that I have big plans but little follow-through. Today I really feel ready to produce."

More applause.

"Anyone else?"

No hands.

"Okay, then," I say. "Today we're going to try to put the whole process together. Actually we started this in yesterday's session, when I asked you to reintroduce the *V* into your practice once you felt comfortable using your mediating thought.

"The combination of mediating thought and the *V* is very powerful. By disrupting old patterns of thinking and feeling, the mediating thought clears your head, which allows you to focus on your targeting. And the focused mindset induced by the *V* should help you implement your mediating thought. They feed into each other.

"Just a quick review of the process: Think your mediating thought just before your opponent hits the ball. Not too soon, though: You don't want to leave time for the old reaction pattern to sneak back in. Then, as soon as your opponent hits the ball, start forming your *V*. If you forget one or the other, that's okay. Just keep trying to work them both in. In time, you'll do it automatically.

"Often the new attitude produced by your mediating thought and your targeting efforts get linked together psychologically. Suppose your MLI is indecisiveness. Your new decisiveness will flow right into wanting to make a decision, and you'll immediately be faced with the decision about what shot to hit off the incoming ball. If your mediating thought has to do with being less passive, your choice of stroke represents an immediate opportunity to be more aggressive. I think you'll find that by linking your mediating thought with your targeting, you'll help both develop. I know that when I'm at the top of my game, I do both almost as one.

"It's great if you can simply think your mediating thought and automatically begin to see your *V*s. That flow reduces your thoughtload to a hop, skip, and a jump away from zoning.

"You may see many different things happening to your strokes at this point in the learning process. Certain strokes may improve dramatically almost immediately; in other strokes, the change may be less dramatic or more gradual. Or at first, although you're feeling good and much less tense, and finding much more pleasure in the game, your strokes actually get worse — everything is sailing long or catching the tape, or your shots are all over the place. Again, this is a temporary setback while your body adapts to the new you.

"And there's the possibility that your new attitude is causing a bit of a war inside of you. Among the most powerful weapons in your old attitude's arsenal are doubt and resistance to change. Suddenly you find yourself thinking that the old way was better, that the new way doesn't work, that you're hitting has gotten worse. Whatever your old attitude throws at you, ignore it. Don't panic. As long as you really like your new attitude and you're making good Vs, your performance will improve. Ultimately, that's how you'll get over all the psychological turmoil: Your performance *will* improve. And when it does, your pleasure in the game is going to grow, and there will be no looking back.

"Understanding the impact of your attitude on your behavior on and off the court is another benefit of this process. For example, when I talk about a major life issue, I'm talking about a personality trait, a persistent aspect of your personality. But sometimes your feelings and behaviors reflect specific circumstances more than the accumulation that is your personality. Psychologists call those mood swings *states*. A state doesn't have the persistence of a trait, but it certainly can affect your game on any given day.

Understanding the psychological bases of problem behaviors and being able to focus on them can give you someplace to look when your game goes astray temporarily. Instead of carrying on about the stiffness in your knees, you might ask yourself why your knees are feeling stiff. Well, it turns out that your knees are a barometer of your involvement: The more involved you are in your game, the easier your knees bend. If you're still thinking about the argument you had with your brother last night, instead of your game, chances are your knees are going to feel stiff. Maybe you ran around all day yesterday, and you're having trouble settling down today. Maybe this particular opponent is intimidating or annoying. Whatever it is, you have a better chance of getting back into rhythm if you know the source of your problem.

"And what do you do about it? Usually you just think your mediating thought and see your Vs, and your game will find itself. But if it doesn't, try a special mediating thought to get you over the rough patch. When I need calming and focusing, I use something like "This one" or "I can do this" to keep my mind on the game. Once I'm feeling better, I tuck that special mediating thought away for another rainy day.

"Coping with opponents. Now that's a major life issue all by itself. But you have the tools you need to overcome the most difficult opponent. To start, ask yourself if there's something about his or her personality that would bother you off the court too. If there is, think about how you would handle this type of person off the court. Suppose you're having a tough day with a "rabbit," a woman who runs everything down. If you met this woman off the court, you would have to be direct with her to get your way. On the court that might translate into being more forceful. What you need then is a mediating thought like "Take this," something to put you in a mindset to be forceful. With your special mediating thought working, you begin to go for your winners, and you find plays like hitting drop shots followed by lobs are effective. Perhaps you begin to serve right at her and then come in to the net. The point is your special mediating thought can keep you steady and focused. Okay, the mindset might not be natural for you, but it's one you can muster for the match and maybe even take a little with you when you leave. These are particularly satisfying experiences. You almost always learn something interesting when you examine yourself in the midst of an awkward situation or facing down a difficult opponent.

Vince Lombardi once said, "If you learn from your mistake, then you haven't really made a mistake." Tennis should provide you with many wonderful learning situations: Just think of the all the mistakes we make on the court. And if you learn from those mistakes, if you use them to uncover facets of yourself you can benefit from both on and off the court, winning or losing a match becomes less important. Even a loss can be satisfying.

"Losing your temper can cost you dearly on the court. Tennis therapy can help you identify the source of your anger and defuse it. Often you're angry at yourself, frustrated that a stroke isn't working or that a shot keeps missing its target. The real problem is not knowing how to fix it, not knowing where to look. Most players don't understand how they play in the first place, even when they're playing well. Now when your game goes off, you know where to look. If you've stopped using your mediating thought, go back to it or create a new one. Use it on every stroke until you feel your attitude changing. Then check your targeting. Frustration comes from feeling that you cannot control or cope with a situation. When you play New Age tennis, you should never feel that way. There's always an answer: You just have to ask the right question.

"New Age tennis also can help build your confidence. Real confidence comes from knowing what you're doing and generally being able to reproduce a behavior. Once you recognize the impact your attitude and powers of concentration have on your play, you should be confident that you can perform well just about any time. And that builds confidence.

"Closely related to confidence is consistency. Think for a moment about all of the sensations that color your life. You can show up on the court angry, distracted, happy, or sad. And once there, you might have a hundred emotional experiences in a match: good shots and bad shots, frustration, doubt, peaks and valleys. New Age tennis gives you a way to play consistently through the turmoil. It's not going to change your experiences: If your opponent makes a bad line call, you're still going to feel cheated. But it can help you control your anger, your frustration, your thoughts of revenge. Just think your mediating thought and see your *V*s, and you'll be focused again on your game.

"Have you ever heard the expression 'Players should play within themselves'? Maybe you've heard a sportscaster or a fan say it about an athlete who's tried a play that isn't part of his or her usual game. You know, when the center on a basketball team throws up a long jump shot and misses badly. To play within yourself in any sport, you must know yourself first. New Age tennis certainly can help you know yourself and design a game that's really you."

Session 6

On the courts, the players are working on fine-tuning their mediating thoughts and being more comfortable with their targeting. The instructors and I are paying special attention to our challenging cases. Marla seems much more into her mediating thought and her targeting. Every now and again, her play begins to be very good. Even she has to admit that when she's doing "it," she hits a good ball. We have her play some points, encouraging her to feel decisive when she thinks "Turtleneck" and then to challenge herself on her Vs by thinking of new targets. When she plays well, she smiles. I know that smile: You can see it on my face whenever I let my body do the swinging nonconsciously and, effortlessly, I hit one just right.

David's overthinking has been quieted somewhat by the V and his mediating thought. We expect good things for him. He's very accepting of the techniques and seems much more relaxed.

Henry's play has been good using the V, but his control issues are keeping him from letting his body play. My sense is that he's only thinking, not feeling, the mediating grunt we gave him — a common problem with controlled types. But we think he can change: The *V* can take so much of players' attention that they "forget" to watch themselves, finding a little freedom from their controlling thoughts. Once they get a feel for that freedom, it's easier for a mediating thought to penetrate. On the agenda: a better mediating thought for Henry. The grunt isn't doing it anymore.

Diane has made great strides with the *V*: She's learning to choose the simple shot, and she's much more focused. But she's doing less well with her mediating thought. She thinks that "Just do the job" is stifling her creativity. After some discussion, we agree that if doing something the simple way works, why not do it? The phrase "Why not?" appeals to Diane. She has a new mediating thought.

Marty is very into both parts of the process. He's coming to realize how much time he spends dreaming and not doing. We're focused now on keeping him from being hard on himself. For a long time, others have been expecting more of him than he's been able or willing to deliver; with the realization that he's been dreaming his way through life has come a tendency to judge himself. Still, he's optimistic about the process.

Lesson 7

READER: **Please join us.**

We begin with a meditation.

I rouse the group after the eighteen minutes is up. "Before we start I want to dispel a myth: There is no winning personality. You don't have to be aggressive, for example, to play better tennis. Somewhere in each of you is a winning personality. It's simply a matter of maximizing your positive qualities and minimizing your negative ones.

"That said, it is true that certain personality traits — aggressiveness, decisiveness, tenacity, competitiveness — make winning easier. If you lack one or more of these qualities, you may feel you're at a disadvantage, and you're right. But you can still play great tennis. The key is to recognize what you're missing and then minimize its impact on your game. The best way to do that is to find a quality you do have that can get the job done.

"Did you ever see Stefan Edberg play? He served and volleyed at a very high level. Although he lived at the net, he wasn't an aggressive player. What he was was very efficient, very steady, and very persistent. And what his play proves is that being aggressive isn't the only way to get to the net

. . . or to win championships. It might help, but it isn't necessary. Other traits — traits that you do have — can get the job done.

"We've spent a good part of this week talking about and working on changing your attitude. But the change we've been talking about is gradual and incremental. You need to be comfortable with yourself and your play. You can't be something you're not, and you shouldn't try. You don't want to be fighting your instincts. That's counterproductive.*

"It's time to think about your good qualities. Don't think about your tennis game now. Think about how you behave and feel off the court. What kinds of things do you do well, and why? What qualities do your family and friends think of when they think of you? What do you like about yourself? Now I'd like you to take a piece of paper and write down five of your good qualities."

I wait a moment or two while the students write.

"Of course, some of your good qualities may not translate well onto the court. Take friendliness, for example. It's a wonderful quality but not in competition. Here's a list of traits that can be useful to you in tennis. Some undoubtedly already are well represented in your game; others less so. Is there one that appeals to you, that you have but would like to develop further? Is there a quality you've always admired in other players?"

I hold up the list and read each item:

* I also believe it can cause injuries on the court.

Aggressiveness	Cunning	Intelligence
Assertiveness	Daring	Persistence
Competitiveness	Decisiveness	Spontaneity
Creativity	Dependability	Tenacity
Courage	Efficiency	Wittiness

"'Okay,' you're saying to yourself. 'I can see how persistence can help on the court. But wittiness?' Actually, laughter, humor, and wit do come into play in tennis. Have you ever seen a witty volley? Of course you have. That's when one player hits a volley behind the other player as she's running toward the open court. Even when you're the victim, you have to laugh.

"I have a friend with a good sense of humor who likes to wind up like he's setting up an overhead and then hit a drop shot with me standing ten feet behind the baseline. Those shots are really witty. Sometimes he actually swings at the ball on its way down, missing intentionally, and then hits a drop shot as the ball rises from its bounce. Risky, eh? Not to him. The shot comes naturally to him. That's the important point. His style matches his personality, and he has learned to maximize his positive qualities. Even a trait as seemingly distant from tennis as wit can be used to improve play.

"*Efficiency* is one entry in the list. Let's say that's your good quality: You like to think of yourself as efficient; you hate wasting anything, including time and energy. You already make use of your efficiency on the court. Most of your strokes are efficient — you swing them with good form and weight transfer, and you get the most out of your swing. But you'd like to improve your serve, your net game, and your approach shots. To do that, you think you need to be more aggressive, but being aggressive doesn't come naturally to you — on or off the court. Oh, you can handle it for the moment it takes to approach a short ball assertively, but then you back off at the last second, or hit a short approach shot or one that floats long. Over time you've started to dread short balls: You never go to the net anymore; sometimes you even retreat to the baseline.

"Clearly your play and your enjoyment of the game are being affected by your lack of assertiveness. But the easy fix — being more aggressive — isn't an option for you. What do you do? You have to design a game that you can be comfortable with. You've already taken the first step: identifying a good quality that works for you on the court, efficiency. Now you want to use that quality to help with specific aspects of your game.

"Let's look at your approach shot, a particularly tough shot for people who aren't aggressive. Instead of bullying yourself to be aggressive, ask yourself, 'What's the most efficient way for me to treat a short ball to, say, my backhand?' Now, go stand on the court about where you would stand if you were hitting an approach shot, and have a practice partner hit a short ball to you. Run in as though you're going to hit your backhand approach shot, but stop just as you swing. Notice where you are. Now look around. Think about being efficient, not aggressive. Forget what everyone has told you, and just look at your options. Look over the net at the other side of the court. You can see more of your opponent's court from where you're standing now than you can from the baseline. Take a step forward. You can see even more. Getting closer is certainly the efficient thing to do. Hitting a ball at the peak of its bounce is also efficient, so part of your strategy is to get in fast to where you can take the ball high on its bounce. Now you decide that it would feel good to hit a short, soft, crosscourt slice on a very wide angle, dragging your opponent off the court on the ad side.*

"Okay, that's a plan. Now go back to the baseline and have your practice partner hit short balls to your backhand. Thinking your mediating thought and seeing your Vs, you try to hit a few soft, wide crosscourt slices off the short balls. Does that shot feel better? Easier? Do you feel more in control? That's playing within yourself.

"Try some more. Have your practice partner feed you short balls and see how it feels to hit efficiently from different spots in the forecourt. Then play out a few points so that you can see what usually follows a wide slice off a short ball."

I hold up a diagram (Figure 12) and show the play as I talk: "Because a short wide slice will run your opponent off the court and forward, he or

* On the player's right as he or she faces the net.

Figure 12
Playing within yourself

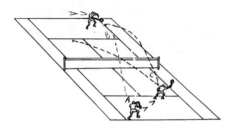

You begin by slicing crosscourt. Your opponent returns up the line, and you cover the shot, tapping a winner into the open court.

she is forced to make a very good return, or your next shot — probably an easy volley into an empty court — is going to end the point.

"What you've done is develop a strategy that makes use of your strength. Volleying into an empty court is a lot easier for you than facing down a passing shot. And you know when you hit a chip-and-charge approach, you stand a good chance of getting a hard passing shot right back at you, which you have to direct effectively or you'll see another one just like it, maybe from even closer range. That takes a certain kind of nerve. But if you hit a wide slice and move in, your opponent is going to run forward and off the side of the court and then try a winner up the line. You cover the angle, and the most you have to do is tap the ball into an open court. Now, that's efficient volleying, not aggressive volleying.

"Does this strategy produce a winning percentage? What percentage were you winning when you were chipping and charging? A good winning percentage going to the net off short balls would be sixty-five percent. Because going to the net is a weakness of yours, let's say you were winning just fifty percent of those shots. I know some very good players who win far less than that off short balls. Maybe with your new strategy, you're winning sixty percent. Well, then, that's *your* winning strategy. You aren't playing by *the* numbers; you're playing by *your* numbers. Your new, efficient style for hitting short balls may never produce the winning percentage of a very good chip-and-charger — say seventy percent — but it's your best play. And if it's natural for you, your percentage playing the

144   LESSON 7

strategy will be higher than that of most people playing the strategy

"Here's what I'm saying. Maybe for an aggressive player, the better percentage play is to hit a deep approach up the line and rush to the net, not to slice wide and give an opponent the chance to hit a running winner. But if the aggressive player's strategy isn't working for you, doesn't feel natural to you, then play *your* best strategy. Even if you win just sixty percent on short balls and your net-charging opponent wins seventy percent on short balls, you haven't lost the game. And it may well be that your personality gives you other advantages. Maybe your nice efficient ground strokes are going to help you win sixty percent of the long baseline rallies. That's the way it works. You want to play naturally and maximize your strengths.

"The important thing is that you manage to get yourself to the net and win a point without the fear you feel when you try to be aggressive. The whole process seems easier. You can relax now on short balls. All you have to do is be efficient, and you can do that. After a while, of course, your opponent is going to be looking for the crosscourt slice, so every now and again you go down the line. That's just what the chip-and-chargers would do, but you're doing it differently, nonaggressively. Your attitude: 'I'm being efficient here because I've got her looking for my crosscourt slice.' In time, your game is gradually going to be more assertive. But in your head, that's not because you're chipping and charging; you're just being more efficient. You've found a more-natural path to the net.

"Do you all see what's happening?" I look around. Most of the students are nodding.

"I want you to pick one of your good qualities and then, when we head to the courts, I want you to go through your whole game. Stand on the court and imagine different strokes. Ask yourself, 'What's the most efficient thing to do, or the most intelligent, or the most dependable?' Then come up with a strategy that uses your strength to strengthen your game.

"The important thing to understand here is that if your mediating thought is doing what it's supposed to do — changing your attitude — the new you isn't going to be comfortable with your old game. You'll feel the need for change in lots of areas but particularly in your choice of shots. You need to find new shots and strategies that reflect your new attitude.

"When you redesign your game, practice your new shots with your mediating thought in mind. Make sure your new strategies fit the new you. Remember your objective is to create a unified experience, a near-zone experience. To meet that objective, your attitude and your play must be compatible.

"Does the game style of the Williams sisters match their personalities? Yes! They are strong and tenacious women. Does John McEnroe's game style match his best qualities? His game is unique, and his style is unlike anyone else's. His game is always direct, creative, and spontaneous, as is he. Doesn't Andre Agassi's style match him? Isn't he exciting just like his game. Look at Pete Sampras: He wins tournaments with solid, reliable play; he's a solid, reliable person.

"So what are you like? Suppose you're the spontaneous type. You never really make plans, but you're pretty good at compensating for your lack of preparation. You think on your feet, and that's a big help. What kind of tennis game would fit you? Well, long baseline rallies clearly don't utilize your skill. You're probably more comfortable hitting winners at the net or applying some tricks to short balls. And you should redesign your game accordingly.

"That process — finding a new game to go with your new attitude — takes a lot of conscious thought during practice. When you find yourself choosing a shot you don't like, stop and ask yourself, 'Would some other shot feel better?' Then try it. Do you like it? Does it fit the new you? Yes? Great! No? Try something else.

"Your focus here should be on comfort and compatibility. Does it feel good? Does it fit well with your mediating thought? Make use of the strokes that come naturally to you. Don't worry if they're low-percentage shots for others. Maybe drop shots come easily to you. Good. Maybe you like to hit wide-angled soft stuff. Well, then, do it. If a stroke comes easily to you and feels right, claim it and use it. The best shot for you is one you're comfortable with, and using that shot can have a dramatic effect on your game.

"An example: Suppose you're getting beat by a good baseliner. To win points, you know you have to get your opponent to the net. What do you do? Let's say that drop shots come naturally to you, so you try three early in the match. Two you hit badly, and they get killed; only one ends up a winner. Is this a losing strategy? Not necessarily. Your opponent clearly is comfortable playing very deep in the court, but he's had to move in a step or two to cover your drop shots. From that position, he's forced to hit all your deep hard stuff on a short hop — something he's not comfortable doing — and his returns are coming back weaker. Now you're dictating the play. Were the three drop shots worth it? Absolutely. Sure, it would have been better to win all three points, but the shot worked: It pulled your behind-the-baseline opponent forward. And if he moves back, you should hit several drop shots again.

"How do you tell that a redesign of your game is in order? Let your play guide you. Watch to see if your game demands any new strokes and if those strokes come naturally to you. If a new stroke seems to create lots of opportunities for your opponents to make you feel uncomfortable, then you need a different game, at least for now. You may grow into the stroke or style, but it isn't you yet. But if your new game is producing new strokes and you like them, wonderful.

"After a long layoff from tennis, I discovered that neither my game nor my mediating thought felt right to me. I did just what I'm telling you to do: I thought about me and which of my characteristics could help my game.

It dawned on me that in the months I hadn't been playing, I'd traveled to Asia and worked on a different-for-me project, and that I had really enjoyed the excitement in my life over that period. My new MLI: living too safely. I began to use the musical theme from *Zorro* as my new mediating thought. It made me less cautious, which matched my new positive characteristic: being more daring. And I set out to design a new game for myself. I began to sneak in to the net off heavy deep topspin. I felt more comfortable hitting a flatter forehand that had more sting on it. I found that I could take loopy stuff out of the air and volley it deep. None of these shots had been part of my old game. And the redesign worked: My game immediately opened up, and the results were very good.

"There was a bonus, of course: I began seeing signs of my newfound daring off the court too. The most important had to do with my career. I had been working with tennis players one on one; now I began to develop and offer workshops to groups of students. And in time, I started The Zone.

"My tennis game plan seems to have become my life game plan. Learning how to get a job done your way is something you take with you when you leave the court. Tennis should be a discovery zone, a testing ground for new ways to further your personal growth.

"Some of you are probably thinking, 'Hey, it's only a game.' But you really can learn a lot from a game. Last week I watched my four-year-old daughter at one of those play areas. She stumbled her way through a room full of colorful plastic balls as the bigger kids rushed past her; climbed a rope ladder along with youngsters who were much more skilled at it; passed through a tunnel high above the ground, which scared her to death; and finally came down a very high slide, which also petrified her. And what did she say the instant she was back on the ground? 'Daddy, I want to do that again.'

"My point: Children learn from every experience, including play. And you should too. Don't just try to master the game. Master yourself; the game will follow."

The instructors walk around the room helping the students choose a positive trait to work on, at least to start. Then we all head outside.

Session 7

We begin by having the students stand at different locations on the court and think out the shot they would like to play. It may be a shot they've always hit or a completely new one. Once they think they have a good stroke, they move to another spot on the court.

Then the instructors begin to feed the students balls at different places around the court. Each student gets lots of practice with each of the strokes he or she selected. As the students hit, the instructors ask them, "How did that shot feel? Good? Was it comfortable? Did you hit it well?" If a student answers no to any of the questions, the instructor reminds the student that he or she is free to try something different.

Before students and instructors take to the courts, I repeat what I've told them about the fit between attitude and game: "In the lesson, I talked about finding your natural game, a game that reflects your new attitude and feels comfortable. Don't be afraid to try a new stroke or a new style. If it's not a good match, try something else. If that doesn't work, you may want to go back and rethink either your mediating thought or the trait you're wanting to strengthen.

"For example, suppose your mediating thought cues you to loosen up your swing. You're going to have a hard time of it if you try to design an assertive, high-powered game. Maybe you've chosen the wrong trait to emphasize. Maybe you should be using more of your creativity. Certainly creativity and a looser, easier style go well together. That's the idea: to find a good match.

"Once you have a game plan, you will become increasingly aware of the shots you want to hit. If you practice those shots, you'll get better at them and you'll use them more. Because your new attitude is in the shot, you'll be reinforcing it with each stroke. And when you leave the court, at least a little bit of that attitude is going to leave with you. That can lead to profound personal discovery and growth."

●

When the session is over, the instructors meet to review the practice. The consensus: Some of the students are still in need of fine-tuning, but most are quickly growing comfortable with the sequences they want to include in their play.

Marty is one of the students with a problem. He's feeling down, not because he's playing badly — he isn't — but because he's come to see that many of the difficulties he faces in life stem from his tendency to dream. The positive trait he wants to develop is flexibility, a great choice. He'd been using his flexibility to adapt to his old attitude: If something fit his image of himself, he took to it; if it didn't, he'd ignore it (just like he ignored his backhand on the court). Now he wants to apply his talent for being flexible to all of his strokes. Although the thought of opportunities missed is making him sad, he's also excited about the potential he's seeing in all of his strokes.

The other four students we've been tracking are doing well. Diane is at the top of her game. She's into creating challenging shots, which seem to be meeting her need for at least a bit of rebelliousness. The trait she wants to emphasize is productivity: She wants to get more out of what she does. Her new game is more assertive, less fanciful. Her targeting skills have become excellent. She is very pleased with herself and her play.

Henry finally has a mediating thought and a positive image to match. His mediating thought — "Dead weight" — is based on an experience he had at the beach. Several friends had teased him, saying he was so muscular, so physically dense, that he would sink. He remembers that the joking actually relaxed him, made him feel loose. Henry's positive quality is efficiency, and he's really good at developing it. He's flattened out his serve and is reaching higher for overheads, so we're pleased.

Even Marla has finally come around. Today she hit several balls over the fence just for the fun of it. She says the game feels different to her now. Her positive trait is intelligence. She told me this morning that she'd been so locked into routine that she wasn't using her smarts to full advantage. We let her play several games and gave her 2 points for every drop-shot winner she initiated, for every rally she won by changing the direction of the rally, and for every smart play (like hitting behind her opponent). More good news: Her energy level has risen along with her self-esteem.

David is like a new player. His mind has quieted, and his focus is sharp. He selected cunning as his positive quality, and he has indeed worked it into his game. He's able to plan a point without thinking it to death. His execution is excellent. Overthinkers tend to do well at The Zone.

That Evening

It's late the last night, and there's a knock at my door. It's Marty asking to talk with me.

"Tonight at dinner, some of the others asked if I wanted to go along with them into town. Before I knew it, I said no, that I had something to do. But I don't really. I think maybe because I didn't want to go, I just said whatever came out of my mouth."

"*Were* you planning to do something tonight?" I ask.

"I was thinking about picking out a video and getting someone to watch it with me."

"Someone?" He smiles to let me know we both understand who that means. He has a crush on one of the girls in the group, and everyone knows it.

"Did you do anything to see to it that your plans for the evening would actually happen?"

"Not really. I mentioned at dinner that I like some of the videos in the library here. I was thinking that maybe someone would sort of pick up on it."

"Marty, you were dreaming again. The trip into town wasn't in your dream, so you ignored it — said whatever you said — and you ended up unhappy. We couldn't ask for a better example of how you play your weaker strokes."

He nods and grins. But then tears well up in his eyes.

"I spend too much time dreaming, don't I?" he asks after a bit.

"I think maybe just not enough time in the moment," I say gently.

Then I let him borrow my car to get into town.

I have to tell you, I live for these moments. They remind me that we change more than tennis games here.

Good-bye

The students are leaving this morning. I've asked them to join me in the classroom one last time. As they walk in, I hand each of them a list, a summary of the process to take with them to the court:

- Begin seeing the Vs, the farther in front of you the better.
- Take a leap of faith and visually jump from ball to V.
- Keep your head down: See the ball with the tops and sides of your eyes.
- Find your major life issue.
- Create a mediating thought to change your attitude.
- Use your strengths to design a new game for yourself.

"Well, it's time to put it all together. For a few weeks, you're going to find it challenging to do all of these things at once. You may want to focus on one at a time. Know that when these lessons are given on a weekly basis, the students get to practice Vs for a week before they're asked to track the ball with their eyes, not their heads. Then they practice that for a week. Only then do we introduce the MLI and the mediating thought.

"Give the process a month, and you won't want to go back to your old style of play. Give it two months, and you won't be able to go back because you will have changed. In fact, your old game won't exist anymore because you're no longer the same person playing it.

"And don't stop there. Once you've got a handle on one MLI, find a new one, create or remember a new mediating thought, and start working again. If you replace one Uh-oh with a good feeling, you've made progress. And when you've replaced a bunch of Uh-ohs, your life will be forever changed.

"Don't forget that growth is a process and that tennis is a means. Your performance on the court reflects much of who you are. Use it that way. Don't be afraid to ask, 'Why am I playing this way?' The answer will be bigger than your tennis game. When you effect change on the court, you effect change everywhere.

"The reason New Age tennis works is that the conditioning — thinking your mediating thought and seeing your Vs — is tied to an activity that you like and that motivates you. Not that repetition isn't a factor. After all, you're working on your attitude and your focus with every shot, as many as a couple of hundred times in a set. But because you enjoy the game, the reward for training — the pride and pleasure you take in playing better —

has all the more meaning. That can only speed the process of permanently altering your behavior on and off the court.

"We started a week ago with a discussion of zoning. That is, after all, the reason you're here, the reason you've been training, to increase the frequency with which you zone. Through zoning, I believe that you learn very quickly that worrying is a waste of time. Of course, saying 'Don't worry' is easy; actually stopping yourself from worrying is not. But the training you've had here, your meditation, and the work you're going to continue to do should keep your worrying to a minimum. I'm not guaranteeing that you'll end up like Caine, but calm is definitely a by-product of living and playing in a zone.

"How does it feel to play in a zone routinely? At first, you're intrigued with the clarity of your stroking. For those of us who haven't been blessed with perfect focus, that's a pleasure in itself. I used to have days when I didn't 'see' a single ball well. Now I might have a stroke or a rally, rarely more. When you use both your mediating thought and your V, at the very least you'll have a near-zone experience with each swing. It may last just an instant, but it's that instant that makes the shot happen.

"Some days you'll find yourself working at the process, working to think your mediating thought and to see the Vs. When that happens, ask yourself why. See if you can't turn the situation into a learning experience. What about this day or this opponent is causing the interference? You've got the skills both to identify the source of the problem and to solve it.

159   GOOD-BYE

Maybe you haven't played in a few weeks, and you're nervous. Maybe you're facing a new opponent, and you want to do really well. Whatever it is, ask why, and the process becomes easier. And you'll learn something new about yourself.

"Early on I said, 'Zoning begets zoning.' Certainly the more you zone, the more likely you are to zone. But why? Here, too, pleasure is a factor. Zoning feels good: the calm, the clarity, the focus, the sense of accomplishment. I think you'll find yourself attracted to other activities that induce the zone state for you. Maybe you'll pick up the violin again; maybe you'll start to paint. Or maybe your driving will change or the way you do your job or the way you wash your dishes. Expect it because it's going to happen. Your game style and your lifestyle are alike; they always have been and always will be. That person playing tennis with new focus has become you. Congratulations, Grasshoppers."

●

With our good-byes said, I watch them board the bus. I'm realist enough to know that in a few days, some will be doing little if any of the training they learned here. They'll think of this as an interesting vacation, and that's fine. Others will stick with the technique for the rest of their playing days, and will find applications of what they've learned here in everything they do for the rest of their lives. The choice, of course, is theirs.

As the bus pulls away, I notice it still isn't fixed. It seems strained to its limits, belching and backfiring, as it makes it to the top of the hill. Then it disappears over the crest, coasting silently away.

GOOD-BYE

Dr. Robert Soloway has a Phd. in Cognitive Psychology from Emory University with specialties in attention, perception, and motor skill behavior. He has been a college instructor for more than 25 years and has been a state ranked tennis player.

Dr. Soloway is available for coaching and speaking engagements.

"Seeing the Ball" a video by Dr. Soloway demonstrates the techniques outlined in this book. The video is $17.99 + s/h.

Dr. Soloway can be reached at rmsolo@comcast.net